The TURNPIKE ROADS
of Leicestershire and Rutland

Arthur Cossons

KAIROS PRESS
Newtown Linford
Leicester
2003

ISBN 1-871344-30-1

First Edition, 2003

Design and Layout by Robin Stevenson, Kairos Press
Body text in Century Schoolbook BT 10.5pt
Printed in Great Britain by Norwood Press, Anstey, Leics.

Front Cover: The Granby Toll House, London Road, Leicester, painted by A J Thornton.
Reproduced courtesy of Mr A Thornton and Leicester City Museums Service

KAIROS PRESS
552 Bradgate Road,
Newtown Linford
Leicester LE6 0HB
Great Britain.

Contents

List of Figures

Foreword

Arthur Cossons (1893-1963) was a Nottinghamshire headmaster with a lifelong interest in local history and, in particular, the development of the system of turnpike roads in England. He was a natural teacher whose profound knowledge and understanding helped innumerable generations of children – and adults too – to gain an understanding and appreciation of their surroundings. He had a deep respect for all that was being achieved in Leicester and Leicestershire in the years after the second world war, especially in the fields of education and museums. Literally thousands of Nottingham children were brought to Leicester, to see what were some of the most outstanding museums in the country outside London, to learn about the Romans at the Jewry Wall, or local history in the Newarke Houses.

It is no accident therefore that his son should start his museum career as a Student Assistant in Leicester City Museums nor that his daughter has spent most of hers in the county record office. We both benefited from going with him on trips into Leicestershire, by bus from Beeston, to explore the history and archaeology of the county, or with the Historical Association excursions that our father led, to places like Kirby Muxloe or Grace Dieu priory.

Arthur Cossons' first publication on roads, Turnpike Roads of Nottinghamshire, appeared in 1934, with a second edition in 1995. By the 1950s he had published Norfolk, Northamptonshire, Warwickshire and Wiltshire and completed the manuscript of Leicestershire and Rutland. This is his text, together with most of the original maps which he drew himself and with which all his works were graced. The text shows some signs of maturation over the half century or so since it was written but rather than edit it or carry out some modest updating it has been published in substantially its original form, as the first comprehensive work on the roads of the two counties. It is, as far as we know, the only outstanding unpublished work that our father wrote. We hope it makes a worthwhile contribution to the understanding of this little known aspect of history and enables readers and researchers to make some sense of the historical geography of the roads of Leicestershire and Rutland.

Neil Cossons
Hilda Stoddart.
January 2003

Hilda and Neil Cossons in 1950, at the Scaddow Tollhouse on the A514, part of the Moira and Gresley turnpike.

LEICESTERSHIRE AND RUTLAND TURNPIKE ROADS

By Arthur Cossons

Introduction

The system of maintaining roads by means of money collected at toll bars from the users was an answer to a problem created by the partial breakdown of an earlier method of administration, which itself was an effort to solve a similar problem. It is therefore necessary to trace in outline the previous conditions in order fully to understand the turnpike system.

During the Middle Ages, the onus of highway repair rested on the manors. The manorial tenantry repaired the roads as they trimmed the hedges and scoured the watercourses. In default they were amerced in the lord's court. Long-distance traffic was mostly horse-borne and, apart from their use in carting the produce of the harvests, wheeled vehicles were comparatively little used – hardly at all in winter except when the land was frostbound. Legally a road was a way. If the way were passable the law was satisfied.

The manorial method of administration, however, fell to pieces as the bondsmen secured their freedom. A rent-paying tenant, recently freed from agricultural service on the lord's land and from fulfilling the various other manorial obligations, was hardly likely to take kindly to a continuance of compulsion by the court leet as to highway repair. At the end of the Middle Ages, the widespread redistribution of land ownership caused by the dissolution of the monastic houses hastened the collapse of local government by the manorial lords and added its quota of difficulty. Soon afterwards, the expansion of trade, due partly to the redistribution of wealth and partly to the efforts of the explorers, began to have its effect on the volume of traffic and its nature.

In places where the court leet had ceased to function, the responsibility for highway maintenance had come to rest on the parish. In the reign of Mary Tudor this was statutorily confirmed by the celebrated Act for the Mending of Highways.[1] This instituted what came to be known as statute labour, the compulsory service on the roads of the teams and carts of the parishioners who had them and the personal labour of those who had not, under the superintendence of an unpaid, annually chosen surveyor of highways or waywarden. The annual work on the roads took place on four days a year, after harvest, a period which was extended to six days by an amending act of a few years later.[2]

The success or failure of these acts depended almost entirely on the conditions within the restricted area of each parish. Outside influence was small and operated chiefly through the general supervisory powers of the local justices. A public-spirited waywarden might be succeeded by one actuated by self interest; a parish with a small area and a good labour supply might have its boundaries coterminous with a sparsely populated parish with many miles of highways within its limits.

Classified according to the way in which internal and external conditions interacted, parishes fell into three main groups. The roads of one parish might all be

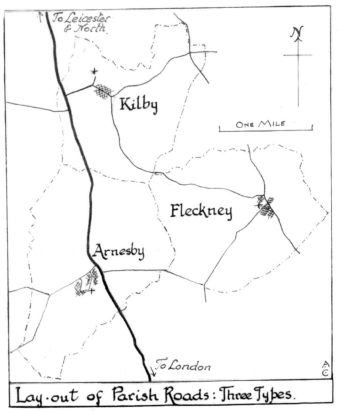

Fig. 1: Roads through Fleckney, Kilby and Arnesby.

In the first of these types, all the roads would get a fair share of the statute labour. It is true that one year's surveyor might pay most attention to those highways that led between his fields and his farmyard but, as all the farmers would take their turn in office, all the roads would get attention, taking one year with another. In the second type, the inhabitants would always be fighting a losing battle, trying their utmost to secure a good highway for their own use and seeing their work set at naught by "foreigners" as soon as it was finished, if not before. It cannot be wondered at that in the third type the parishioners neglected the main road entirely unless a passing magistrate chose to present the parish at the next sessions. A sketch map of three Leicestershire parishes (figure 1) is included to illustrate this point. The roads of Fleckney are seen to be of more or less equal importance, more to the inhabitants and less to the outside traveller. One of the roads radiating from the centre of Arnesby can be seen to be of similar use to the locality as the rest but, being a part of one of the main roads from London to the north, also of importance to the non-parishioner. The same road passes along one side of Kilby and is easily seen of be of far more use to the long distance traveller than to the persons responsible for its repair.

But there was yet another condition that had a great deal of influence on the success or failure of statute labour – the geological structure of the land over which the highways passed. Porous sandstone and limestone meant easy road maintenance. Where a clay subsoil coincided with a road pattern such as those of the second and third types, maintenance was hopeless. Ruts might be raked flat and stones dumped on the surface but the first vehicle after the first rainstorm would bring the mud squelching up between the stone to spread itself over them. Before long, the stones would be sunk in a sea of mud.

regularly used by the inhabitants and hardly at all by strangers. In another, a road of local importance, necessary for the day to day business of the parishioners, might also form a part of a great trunk route and be worn and torn by the passing through of travellers whose statute labour was due elsewhere. Yet again, a main road might pass across the corner of a parish or along its boundary, might be cut to pieces by travellers with no interest in the village at all, be of no value to the parishioners themselves, and yet be reparable by them.

Highway rates were introduced during the Commonwealth when the justices were allowed to pass assessments up to a shilling in the pound.[3] The parish (some townships and chapelries had separate highway jurisdiction) was still the unit of administration. The Cromwellian legislation was of course annulled at the Restoration, but the principle of rating for road repairs was reintroduced soon afterwards but only up to a limit of sixpence in the pound.[4] Many parochial waywardens availed themselves of this opportunity to pay for labour additional to that provided by statute duty, but it did not go very far. Practically the only other sources of income that the surveyor had were the produce of fines for the breaking of various highway laws, money paid in lieu of doing statute labour, and (this was very similar to the last) fines for non-performance. Occasionally a record is found of another way of raising money. A parish would be presented or indicted at the Sessions for non-repair and fined a substantial sum, sufficient to cover the cost of the necessary work. The ratepayers would have to pay the fine in the ration of their assessments and, being a fine and not a rate, it could exceed the statutory sixpenny limit. Once collected, the money would be handed over to the parish surveyor and, the work done, a justice's certificate would ensure a clean sheet at the next sessions. The usual procedure when a parish was indicted was for the case to be respited from sessions to sessions until the work was done and a justice's certificate granted. The parish would then be fined a nominal sum and the case cleared.

Forerunners of the Turnpike System

In the Middle Ages there had been cases of tolls being granted by royal letters patent for the upkeep of bridges (pontage), town streets and short stretches of highway (pavage). They were usually for short periods and, although they were sometimes renewed, the procedure can only be considered as temporary.

Records of these pontage and pavage grants and of the occasional institution of enquiries into the management of the tolls are to be found in the *Calendars of Letters Patent* in the Public Record Office. One local case of pontage must suffice as an illustration. On 12 February 1316, Edward II granted three years' pontage to Robert de Eccleshale and Robert, son of Ivo de Keggeworth, in aid of the bridge of "Keggeworth".[5] Later in the same year he made a fresh grant for the same bridge to the same Robert son of Ivo, this time associated with Hugh de Fisshlake and Geoffrey de Byngham, for five years.[6] Long before its term was run another grant was for four years, this time to Gervase son of Gervase de Clifton, Stephen le Haut of Kegworth and Walter de Brampcote.[7] Three months later the king issued a commission to audit the accounts of the holders of the grant of all money received "as well the gifts of divers men in their testaments as the proceeds of the pontage".[8] A further audit was instituted in 1321.[9]

The Birth of the Turnpike System

For the real beginning of the turnpike system we must come down to much later times. Towards the middle of the seventeenth century, attempts were made by the gentry of Bedfordshire to obtain powers to levy tolls on the local sections of the Great North Road and Watling Street.[10] They failed but similar attempts in neighbouring counties produced the first Turnpike Act, in 1663, which gave the justices of Hertfordshire, Huntingdonshire and Cambridgeshire power to erect gates and charge tolls on traffic passing along the Great North Road in those counties.[11] This Act expired as far as it related to Huntingdonshire and Cambridgeshire, but was renewed for Hertfordshire twice before its precedent was followed in 1695-6.

Thereafter there was a steady stream of bills before Parliament respecting various isolated stretches of highway. When the Stuart period closed with the death of Queen Anne, acts had been passed for over two dozen lengths of road. Most of the earlier ones had been renewed; a few had expired.

Meanwhile in the session 1706-7, a departure from the original type had been made. Two acts passed in that session appointed as road authorities, not the local justices, but bodies of local gentlemen interested in the particular roads as trustees or commissioners.[12] The initiative was local. Local people subscribed funds for the legal costs of petitions to Parliament and, on their bills being passed, they became the "foundation members" of the trusts.

In 1721-2 the turnpike system reached Leicestershire's southern border, but before considering its development in the county and in Rutland, it may be well to quote a few descriptions of the roads as they were prior to turnpiking and in the early years of the system.[13]

Descriptions of the Roads

Writing at about the time of the first Leicestershire turnpike act, Daniel Defoe says,

> … the soil of all the midland part of England, even from sea to sea, is of a deep stiff clay, or marly king, and it carries a breadth of near 50 miles at least, in some places much more; nor is it possible to go from London to any part of Britain, north, without crossing this clayey dirty part.[14]

After describing the Great Northern Post Road from London to York "with its famous Arrington Lanes" and "Tuxford in the Clays", he goes on,

> Suppose you take the other northern road, namely, by St. Albans, Dunstable, Hockley, Newport Pagnel, Northampton, Leicester and Nottingham, or Derby: On this road, after you are pass'd Dunstable, which, as in the other way, is about 30 miles, you enter the deep clays, which are so surprisingly soft, that it is perfectly frightful to travellers, and it has been the wonder of foreigners, how, considering the great number of carriages which are continually passing with heavy loads, those ways have been made practicable; indeed the great number of horses every year kill'd by the excess of labour in these heavy ways, has been such a charge to the country, that new building of causeways, as the Romans did of old, seems to me to be much easier expense: From Hockley to Northampton, thence to the very bank of Trent these terrible clays continue; at Nottingham you are pass'd them, and the forest of Sherwood yields a hard and pleasant road for 20 miles together.[15]

In a later passage, after describing the improvements made by turnpiking some of the roads in the southern half of England, he writes,

> There are indeed some very deep roads in many places of England, and that south by Trent too, where no such provision is yet made for repair of the roads, as particularly in and through the vale of Aylesbury, … also beyond Northampton to Harborough and Leicester; also in Lincolnshire, … the road from Stamford to Grantham, Newark, and Tuxford in the clays, all which remain very deep, and in some seasons dangerous.[16]

From the petitions to Parliament and the preambles of the early turnpike acts can be collected a variety of expressive descriptive words and phrases. Roads were "deep and foundrous", "ruinous and bad", "narrow and incommodious", "a Coach with eight Horses cannot pass ... without great Difficulty", "three Pack-horses down in the Road at the same Time", "two Carriages cannot pass each other", "totally impassable even for a single Horse with Safety".

William Marshall, nearly at the end of the eighteenth century, describes the road between Nottingham and Loughborough.[17] After a dissertation on the merits of flat, convex and concave surfaces, he writes,

> The road between Nottingham and Loughborough is held out, by the advocates of hollow ways, as a specimen of their good effect.

> This road, however, though much flatter than modern roads in general are, is by no means uniformly reduced to the principle and form contended for: indeed, a part, which has lately been made, is thrown into the barrel form: a strong evidence that the trough principle, in this instance, is growing into disrepute. Taking it altogether, in its present state ... and considering the materials, an excellent gravel, and the publicness of the thoroughfare to pay for the forming and repairs, the part I saw of it, between Trent Bridge and the top of Bunny Hill, may, without prejudice, be deemed one of the worst-kept roads in the kingdom. The steeps torn into inequalities, and the levels loaded with mud to the footlocks. The more gentle slopes, though uneven, harsh, and unpleasant to travel upon, were certainly not indictable: a proof that on such surfaces, and with such materials, roads may be kept in a travelable state, in defiance of running water.

> ...had the materials been put into a better form, they would have afforded a better road...

Every part of the journey from Leicester to London bore ample testimony of the superiority of the CONVEX PRINCIPLE; and I have no longer any doubt of the propriety of forming a public carriage road, moderately round, with an open channel on either side, as a horse path; with banks, level on the top, as guards to these paths, and as resources, in wet weather, for foot passengers; and (where the width of the lane will permit) with a side road for summer travelling.[18]

Of the Tamworth to Ashby Road,[19] he says that until some twenty years previously, it

> lay in a state almost impassable, several months in the year. Statfold Lane had long been proverbial. In winter it was unfrequented; the riding and driftways, at least being on trespass, thro the adjoining inclosures. Wagons were dragged on their bellies through it: to a coach it was impassable, during the winter months: and might still have lain in that state, had not a material, which is seldom used in this intention, been applied to its amendment: namely, SAND ...[20]

Writing about the same time, John Monk shows that the concave road was favoured by the two rural reformers, Robert Bakewell of Dishley and Joseph Wilkes of Seal.[21] The roads past Dishley and through Measham were both on this principle and "certainly in much better order than the roads about them". The road through Breedon had also been influenced by Wilkes and this was better than ever remembered and less expensive to maintain. Monk says that opinion in the county generally was divided among the concave, convex and perfectly flat principles. Some of the convex roads had been made so high in the middle as to be dangerous. The turnpike roads of the county as a whole were "tolerably good" but would be "much better if it were not for the very heavy narrow wheeled wagons which are employed in the carriage of lime and coals", some of which carried five tons each.

The non-turnpike roads were "in many parts of the county infamously bad". The roads were sometimes nothing more than rights of way through fields on the turf, which bore no trace of wheels for miles together. It was impossible to take a carriage on to some of them and when riding there was an intolerable number of gates to open.

It seems that the idea behind the concave road was that on slopes the rain washed all the loose stones and grit down and left the road surface clean, but, as Marshall says about Bunny Hill, theory did not always work out in practice. On level roads, artificial slopes were introduced to have the same effect. Gaps in the roadside banks were made at the foot of each slope to allow the water to run off but, again as Marshall points out, the mud collected where it should have been carried off.

Leicestershire and Rutland

As stated above, the turnpike system reached the southern border of Leicestershire in 1721-2. In that session was passed an Act for placing under the control of trustees two roads northwards from the outskirts of Northampton. One reached the county boundary at Welford Bridge and the other at what was then the boundary at the Chain Bridge, Market Harborough.[22] Four years later, the latter route to the north was extended by the turnpiking of the road from Market Harborough to Leicester and on to Loughborough.[23] Twelve more years passed before the toll system was extended to a further continuation when, in 1737-8, Acts were passed for two routes

Fig. 2: Bitteswell Toll Gate and Cottage, from a lithograph of the 1840s.

Fig. 3: The toll house at Lount, near Ashby-de-la-Zouch.

northwards from Loughborough, one to Derby via Wilne or Wilden Ferry and beyond to Ashbourne, Brassington, and halfway to Buxton,[24] the other (with a gap from Loughborough to Cotes Bridge) to Nottingham.[25] In the following year Rutland was reached and crossed, by the turnpiking of the Great North Road between Stamford and Grantham.[26]

The further development in the two counties can best be studied by reference to the list of acts and roads in the Gazetteer and to the accompanying notes and maps. The notes are not claimed to be exhaustive. In fact they only give, with few exceptions, the barest outline of routes and dates. For the histories of the individual trusts, it is necessary to examine the minute and account books as has been done by Mr Percy Russell in his story of the Market Harborough and Loughborough road.[27] Many of these sources of information are now lost; many are stored away in the offices of solicitors whose predecessors acted as trustees' clerks; some are, fortunately, finding their way into the custody of reference libraries and the muniment rooms of local authorities. The Record Office at Leicester has thus acquired a fairly large collection of acts, books, maps and other documents relating to county roads. An annual statement of accounts for each trust in each county would have been in the custody of the Clerk of the Peace at every county town. These could cover the years between 1822 and the extinction of the trusts.[28] There may also be a file of answers to a questionnaire sent to all trusts in 1820, giving particulars of length of road, cost of repairs, amount of revenue, rate of interest on bonded debt and the amount of debt.[29]

A few general notes on the area as a whole may be useful in addition to the notes on the separate roads in the Gazetteer. There is no case in the district of a trust controlling all the roads radiating from one town. This is general throughout the Midlands and the North. In the South-West there were many cases of radiating roads controlled by one trust. All or nearly all the roads radiating from, for example, Bath, Bristol, Devizes, Poole, Bruton, Westminster and Frome were thus grouped. In the case of Bristol, the original Act covered twelve roads centring on the city, and by gradual lengthening and the addition of cross roads, the trust eventually came to be the largest in the country, with a mileage of 180.[30] On the other hand, there were seven trusts operating nine roads radiating from Leicester.

Passing a Turnpike Act through Parliament

As a specimen of the steps taken, the following summary of the first Act for Hinckley to Woeful Bridge, etc., road (no.18) may be of interest.

On 21 January 1760 a petition was presented to the House of Commons from various "Gentlemen, Clergy and principal inhabitants of the County of Leicester", stating that the roads from "the Guide Post in Duck Paddle Street, Hinckley,...are in a very founderous Condition, and in many Parts thereof, in the Winter Season, are impassable for Wheel Carriages, without great Difficulty;...that there are several very large Collieries and Lime Works near the said Roads", and asking for powers to levy tolls so that "Coals and Lime at all Times of the Year and at a reasonable Price" could be available.

On 5 February, Mr Henry Eames surveyor, was examined and stated that the roads were "in the Winter Season so deep, that they are not passable for Carriages; that they are in many places too narrow;...". There were five collieries and many lime pits in the neighbourhood. Leave was given to bring in a bill. This was read a first time on 11 February and a second time on 18 February, when it was sent to Committee.

It was agreed on 20 February that "all were to have Voices who came to the Committee", that is, that the committee was thrown open for any M.P. who wished to attend and vote. Possibly this was because the petitioners' friends were expecting opposition and used this method of defeating it. In any case, two opposing petitions were presented on 22 February and they were referred to the committee already considering the first petition. One was from William Wollaston, Esq., owner of coal mines in Measham, who asked to be heard as the bill, if passed, would be detrimental to his interests and give unfair advantage

to the mines in Cole Orton and Swannington. The second was from several persons who alleged that part of the road between Hinckley and Osbaston would be parallel to another included in a bill then pending (Burton Bridge To Market Bosworth, etc., see no.19), that is the road from Hinckley through Dadlington, Market Bosworth and past Hoop Hall, to Belchiers. The latter road, said the petitioners, would be much more useful and they foresaw that with traffic divided between the two roads, tolls on both would be

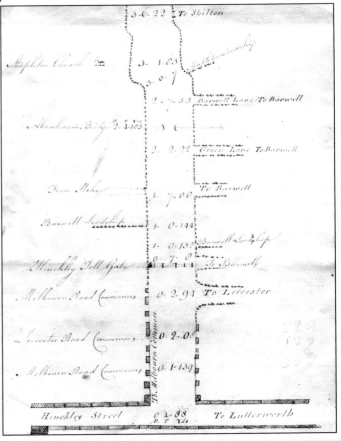

insufficient to repair both. They therefore asked that the road from Hinckley to Belchiers be omitted from the bill.

On 5 March, a further petition asked for the inclusion of the roads between Breedon Brand and Woeful Bridge, via Redwood Lane, and through Gelscoe Lane to Diseworth Field.

The next day, in the report stage, the bill was recommitted with instructions to the committee to make provision for the last mentioned alterations. The bill was reported again on 12 March and passed on 21 March. The Lords signified their assent on 1 April and on 15 April, the Royal Assent was notified. (HCJ vol. 28, relevant dates)

The Redwood Lane part of the roads included in the petition of 5 March seems to have been adopted as the main road in the Act, instead of whatever was intended by the original petition to be the way between Breedon Brand and Woeful Bridge. The Belton Turn which terminated the Gelscoe Lane branch of the Act seems to have been the second turn towards Belton, which is at the Diseworth boundary, thus conforming to the 5 March petition

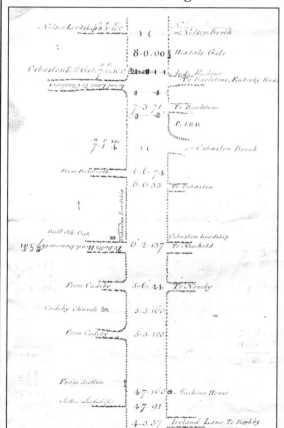
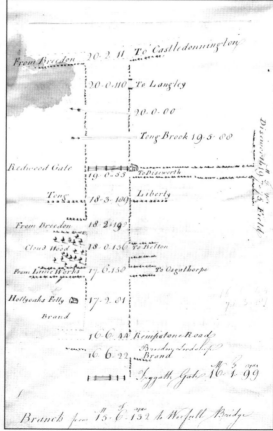

Fig. 4: Plans of parts of the Hinckley Road surveyed in 1796 by James Holworthy:

(a) (opposite page) Hinckley to Stapleton;

(b) (centre) Osbaston Gates;

(c) (right) Cloud Wood sections.

For a detailed map of this turnpike see page 54.

The five turnpike roads centring on Market Harborough were all independent, while six bodies of trustees managed the seven roads meeting at or on the outskirts of Hinckley. It should be stated however that, though operating under separate Acts, many of the trusts consisted largely of the same members and with the same clerk.

A feature fairly common in the Midlands was that of one trust operating one long stretch of road that proved unwieldy and had to be divided. For example, the road from Loughborough to the county boundary at Wilne Ferry was originally a part of a system that went on to Derby and then forked, one branch going to Ashbourne and Hurdloe House, and the other to Hulland Ward and Brassington.[31] This eventually became three separately-managed trusts.

Similarly, the Leicestershire to Coventry road trust originally had under its control the road from Leicester through Hinckley and Nuneaton to Coventry, its continuation through Warwick to the south of Warwickshire at Halford Bridge, a long branch to Stratford on Avon, and shorter branches from Coventry to the Stoneleigh boundary and from Leicester to Narborough.[32] This eventually became four trusts. The long Nottingham to Kettering road, on the other hand, was always administered as one trust, though divided into districts.[33] Each division had its own trustees' meetings but they all carried out the same acts of Parliament, and had occasional joint meetings.

Perhaps the most striking feature shown by the turnpike maps is the density of trust-controlled roads in the west of Leicestershire due, of course, to the existence of the coalfield. Most of the development in that area occurred in the ten years following 1753. Before that year there was no turnpike road in Leicestershire south of the Loughborough to Derby road and west of Leicester. That year saw the turnpiking of the main road through Ashby in two sections, Leicester to Ashby[34] and Ashby to Tutbury.[35] In the following year, Hinckley and Nuneaton were connected with the county town,[36] and in 1756-7 Ashby was connected with Loughborough,[37] and the Charnwood Forest road was added.[38] Nearly all the remainder of the roads turnpiked in the west of the county, with Measham and Coleorton as central foci, became controlled between 1759 and 1762. The

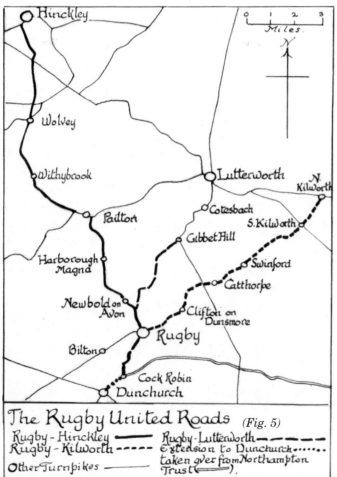

The Rugby United Roads (Fig. 5)

Rugby-Hinckley ———
Rugby-Kilworth -----
Other Turnpikes ———
Rugby-Lutterworth — — —
Extension to Dunchurch ·······
taken over from Northampton Trust (————)

Desford road (1787-8)[39] and the Moira and Gresley group (1794, with later extensions)[40] were practically all the roads in the coalfield area added later than 1762. In Nottinghamshire, the development of turnpikes on the coalfield occurred very slightly later, beginning in 1758.[41]

Very few important roads in the two counties of Leicester and Rutland remained outside the turnpike system altogether. The Fosse Way between Saxondale, near Bingham, and Syston, and between Stoney Stanton and Brinklow was never turnpiked, and neither was the section of Watling Street between High Cross and Gibbet Hill.

Construction and Maintenance

Pre-turnpike repair methods were primitive in the extreme. Turnpiking did not, at first, alter the methods, but improvement was certainly accomplished, as Defoe's remarks on roads in the south of England testify.[42] The trustees' surveyors were, like parochial waywardens, untrained, but their appointments were not annual. They were able to learn by trial and error, by experience spread over more than one round of the seasons. More important was the fact that they had more money to spend. They could do what the parish surveyors did but at more frequent intervals, for they could hire labourers, they could buy stone as well as dig in the common lands near the road and, for a turnpike act did not generally exempt the parishioners, they could have a share of the statute labour as well or a money payment in lieu.

Progress was, however, very slow and haphazard but, here and there, an individual trustee or magistrate would devote a similar amount of energy and time to his work as a road commissioner as he did to estates or to his duties on the bench. Occasionally during the latter half of the eighteenth century we hear of such men, but their work was restricted in scope and local in its application. During that period, however, two men were growing up who were to bequeath their name to history for the work they did after the turn of the century.

Thomas Telford (1756-1836) had, when the nineteenth century came in, already made a name as a civil engineer with many works to his credit – harbours, docks, canals and public buildings.[43] In 1810 he undertook a government survey of the roads from London to the north-west and from 1815 onwards was

Fig. 6: Proposed road from Coventry to near Stoney Stanton, surveyed by E. Philips in 1830.

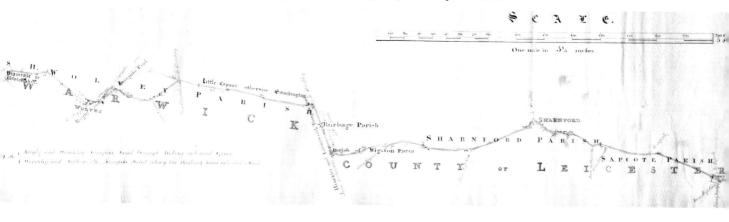

in charge of realigning and regrading the Holyhead road,[44] a work which led to the construction of his greatest monument, the Menai Suspension Bridge.[45] His work was chiefly concerned with road engineering. His method of surfacing was (apart from the modern use of tar or bitumen) much like that used today. The upper layers were of small broken stone laid on a foundation of large hand-set stones.

John Loudon McAdam (1757-1834) was not at first a professional engineer or surveyor. After some years in posts connected with the Admiralty, he settled in Bristol and become a trustee of the great Bristol Trust. In 1816 he resigned to take up the general surveyorship under the same trust. To him, foundations did not matter. His roadway had to be well drained and on it laid a ten-inch layer of stone broken to a uniform size (each piece weighing about six ounces) and united by their own angles under pressure of the traffic.[46] McAdam's enemies called his roads "elastic".[47] He himself said that, other than actual bog, he preferred a soft base to a rocky one. To turnpike trustees the great advantage of his method was its cheapness. Lifting the old material right out, screening it and breaking the larger stones to McAdam's stipulated size, often resulted in the trustees not merely avoiding the purchase of new material but having some left over.

McAdam severed his connection with the Bristol Trust after a few years and became a consultant surveyor. When called upon to advise he usually stipulated the appointment of a sub-surveyor of his own training to supervise the work. Many young men who had gained their experience under McAdam in work for the Bristol and other west country trusts were thus placed in charge of relaying operations up and down the country. His own three sons and a grandson were also in the business.[48] His second son, James Nicoll McAdam, was eventually knighted when general surveyor to the trust operating a union of the roads leading out of London north of the Thames – a union effected in 1826.[49]

Speed

Perhaps the greatest tribute to the work of these two great roadmakers is that contained in the time-tables of the Royal Mail coaches. In 1784, John Palmer of Bath instituted the carriage of mails by coach instead of by mounted postboys. In that year the first mail coach ran from Bristol to London at seven miles an hour. Perhaps local examples will be more interesting. At the beginning of the nineteenth century the mails travelling on Leicestershire and Rutland roads were the following:

London to
(a) Holyhead, via St Albans, Northampton, Lutterworth, High Cross, Hinckley, Atherstone, Tamworth, Lichfield, Stafford, Chester and Bangor Ferry.
(b) Carlisle, via Northampton, Market Harborough, Leicester, Loughborough, Derby and Manchester.
(c) Carlisle and Glasgow, via Hatfield, Stevenage, Stamford, Grantham, Newark, Doncaster and Boroughbridge.
(d) Berwick and Edinburgh, via Ware, Huntingdon, Norman Cross, Stamford, Grantham, Doncaster, York and Newcastle.
(e) Leeds, via Welwyn, Bedford, Kettering, Oakham, Melton Mowbray, Nottingham, Mansfield and Sheffield.

The coaches left London at 8 p.m. The following table shows the arrival times at some local towns for 1811, with the hourly mileage.[50]

	Arrive	Miles	Speed m.p.h.
Leicester	10.20 a.m.	98	6.83
Loughborough	12.50 p.m.	109	6.47
Lutterworth	9.09 a.m.	89	6.84
Hinckley	10.40 a.m.	99½	6.78
Stamford	7.35 a.m.	89	7.68
Oakham	11.00 a.m.	94¾	6.31
Melton Mowbray	12.30 p.m.	104¾	6.34

There were some rearrangements in the 1820s, the chief being the transfer of the Holyhead mail to Telford's newly reorganised road via Daventry, Coventry, Birmingham and Shrewsbury, the old route through Hinckley and Atherstone being continued for the Chester mail which was then extended to Woodside Ferry, Birkenhead, for Liverpool.

In 1835 the mails using roads in the two counties were those from London to

(a) Glasgow via Welwyn, Stamford, Grantham, Newark, Orton, Worksop and Boroughbridge.
(b) Chester and Woodside Ferry, via Northampton, Welford, Lutterworth, Hinckley, Atherstone and Tamworth.
(c) Leeds, via Welwyn, Bedford, Kettering, Oakham, Melton Mowbray, Nottingham, Mansfield and Sheffield.
(d) Carlisle and Portpatrick, via Northampton, Market Harborough, Leicester, Loughborough, Derby and Manchester.
(e) Berwick and Edinburgh, via Ware, Huntingdon, Stamford, Grantham, Doncaster, York and Newcastle.

Fig. 7: The toll gate on Leicester's London Road, from a postcard dated 1878

At this period, after the work of Telford and McAdam had been done and before the coming of the railway had had an adverse affect, the speeds were:[51]

	Arrive	Miles	Speed m.p.h.
Mkt Harborough	4.37 a.m.	85	9.86
Leicester	6.03 a.m.	99	9.85
Loughborough	7.30 a.m.	110	9.56
Lutterworth	5.30 a.m.	90	9.47
Hinckley	6.36 a.m.	101	9.52
Melton Mowbray	6.57 a.m.	106	9.68
Oakham	5.55 a.m.	96	9.68
Stamford			
(Edinburgh Mail)	5.15 a.m.	86	9.29
(Glasgow Mail)	5.28 a.m.	89	9.40

A new mail to Halifax via Market Harborough, Leicester, Nottingham, and Sheffield, was timed to do the following speeds in the next year:[52]

	Arrive	Miles	Speed m.p.h.
Mkt Harborough	4.23.a.m.	83	9.90
Leicester	5.48 a.m.	98	10.00
Loughborough	6.50 a.m.	109	10.06

It will be noticed that the mileage differs slightly in the two sources.

These later speeds, it must be remembered, were not mere figures in a time-table but were actually maintained, except in very adverse circumstances. The increase in speed between 1811 and 1835 for the towns listed was over 40 per cent.

In the time-table for the next year[53] appeared notice of the carriage of mails between Birmingham and Warrington, Liverpool and Manchester by the Grand Junction[54] and Liverpool and Manchester[55]

Railways. The first steam-operated railway south of the Trent had already been open some years between Leicester and Swannington,[56] and a number of horse-traction lines also existed in the county and on its borders.[57] The Midland Counties Railway connecting Rugby, Leicester, Derby and Nottingham, was under construction.[58] What Sir James McAdam called "the calamity of railways" had occurred.

Vehicles and Horses

Right through the turnpike period there was continuous conflict between the users of the roads and those responsible for their maintenance. The highway authorities attempted to make the traffic conform to the roads by restrictions of four types – on weights of lading, on width of wheels, on shape of tyres and on the number of beasts of draught.

These restrictions began to appear before the turnpike system was inaugurated and afterwards continued on two parallel lines, a series of General Highways Acts, applicable to the roads kept up by the parishes, and a series of General Turnpike Acts, applicable to all turnpike roads, irrespective of the regulations laid down for each trust in its local act. In 1654 no cart or waggon could be drawn by more than five horses or six oxen and a horse, except that any number could be used for drawing millstones and timber in the summer months.[59] No waggon was to have wheels less than four inches in width from 1662, when it was also enacted that waggons travelling for hire laden should have seven horses (six to be paired) or less, or eight oxen, or six horses and two oxen.[60] Eight years later five horses only could be used if harnessed in file, but more if in pairs.[61] Poles between the wheel-horses or else double shafts had to be fitted, under an Act 1695-6,[62] while in 1706-75 the upper limit of the number of horses was reduced to six, although

Types of Vehicle Listed in Toll Schedules of Turnpike Acts

Passenger Vehicles, (also including Light Goods Vans, etc.)

Barouche	Chaise	Hearse	Sledge
Berlin	Chaise Marine	Landau	Sociable
Break	Chariot	Landaulet	Stage Coach
Calash	Coach	Litter	Tax Cart
Car	Curricle	Market Cart	Taxed Cart
Caravan	Diligence	Phaeton	Van
Cartree	German Waggon	Post Chaise	Vis-à-Vis
Chair	Gig		Whiskey

Goods Vehicles

Cart	Dray	Tumbril	Wain
Curry	Drug	Timber Carriage	
Drag	Gill	Waggon	

Of course, this list includes more than one name for the same type of vehicle. Even so, there were other names not listed above and not found in turnpike acts by the writer, e.g. cabriolet, waggonette, briska, brougham, dog cart, stanhope, tilbury.

Fig. 8: A family coach of 1820s in Snibston Discovery Park

The Tax Cart or Taxed Cart was an early nineteenth century 'utility' or 'austerity' vehicle. Under the 'war budgets' of Napoleonic times high taxes were levied on carriages, but for the benefit of the 'little man' exemptions from the full taxation were granted to the owners of carts built to a specification contained in the tax schedules. Under the Act of 1803 the Taxed Cart paid a tax of £1 4s. instead of five guineas payable for other one horse, two wheeled carriages. The specifications of a Taxed Cart were that it must be

built and constructed wholly of Wood and Iron, without any Covering other than a tilted Covering, and without any Lining or Springs, whether the same be made of Iron, Wood, Leather, or other Materials, and with a fixed Seat, without Slings or Braces, and without any Ornament whatever, other than Paint of a dark Colour for the Preservation of the Wood or Iron only, and which shall have the Words "A Taxed Cart", and the Owner's Christian and Surname, and Place of Abode, marked or painted on a Black Ground in White Letters, or on a White Ground in Black Letters, on the Outside of the back Pannel or back Part of such Carriage, in Words at full Length, each of the Letters thereof being at least one Inch in Length, and of a Breadth in Proportion, and the Price of which (Repairs Excepted) shall not have exceeded, or the Value thereof shall not at any Time exceed the Sum of twelve Pounds Sterling, which shall be kept by any Person or Persons for his, her, or their own Use, and not for Hire.

the justices could specify certain hills in their counties for which the number could be increased.[63]

The rose-headed nail came in for censure in 1719.[64] No waggon with them in tyres could be drawn by more than three horses and the same applied to wheels with strakes less than 2½ inches wide. (See Figure 9)

In 1741 the weighing engine put in an appearance on turnpike roads, with extra tolls for weights above certain limits,[65] and seven years later a loophole was covered by laying down penalties for carters who partially unloaded their vehicles on one side of a toll-rate and reloaded beyond it.[66] The leading through the gates of horses above legal numbers and reharnessing on the other side received attention in 1751.[67]

The so-called first Broad Wheel Act was passed in 1753. By this no waggon was allowed on turnpike roads with wheels less than nine inches in width, except those drawn by oxen or by less than five horses. Any number of horses up to eight could be used with broad wheels without overweights being charged.[68]

The second Broad Wheel Act, two years later, allowed three years' exemption from tolls for waggons with nine-inch wheels, and five years was added to the term of the local act of any trust which increased the tolls on narrow-wheeled vehicles.[69]

As to the shape, the 1755 Act stipulated that in order to benefit, broad wheels had to be cylindrical and not conical. The conical wheel, especially when the vehicle was turning, ground the roads, the cylindrical wheel rolled them. The full-width wheel with three strakes, the middle one projecting, also incurred the displeasure of the authorities for such wheels ran on middle strakes, having the effect of a narrow wheel. In 1762, preferential treatment at the toll-bars was given to waggons with the fore and hind

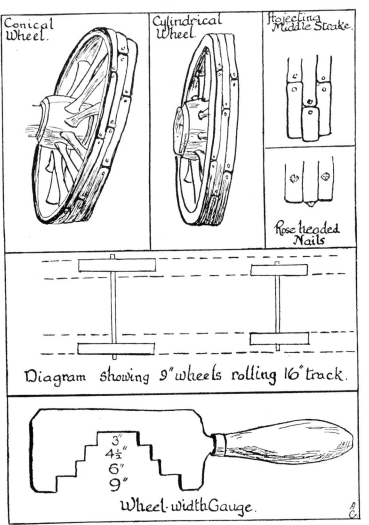

Fig. 9: Wheel design and construction.

Conical Wheel.

Cylindrical Wheel.

Projecting Middle Strake.

Rose headed Nails

Diagram showing 9" wheels rolling 16" track.

3"
4½"
6"
9"

Wheel-width Gauge.

wheels so placed that together they rolled a 16-inch track.[70] Five years' exemption from toll were allowed from 1774[71] for waggons with 16-inch rollers but it is doubtful if many of the monsters of the waggon builders' craft ever took to the roads.[72]

Tolls

Perhaps in no particular do turnpike acts differ more than in the schedules of tolls to be charged. It is certainly true that foot passengers were always free, but the charges for animals and vehicles vary between fairly wide limits. Tolls also vary in the way they are stated.

Some trusts made an "all round" charge for all classes of vehicles or all horses drawing them. Others differentiated between passenger and goods vehicles or between four- and two-wheeled carriages. Most trusts, in their middle and later stages, varied the tolls according to wheel-width. In the specimen toll schedules given on pages 22-23, the full descriptions are not given in order to save space. "Carriage etc." can be taken to mean a sprung passenger carriage. "Waggon etc." means a four-wheeled goods vehicle. "Cart etc." means a two-wheeled goods vehicle. In the actual schedules from which these summaries have been compiled, the descriptions are much fuller, for example one might find the following:

For every Horse, Mare, Gelding, Mule or other Beast.[73] drawing any Coach, Chariot, Landau, Berlin, Hearse, Chaise, Calash, Waggon, Wain, Cart, or other Carriage, of any Name or Description, the Sum of Three Pence.

Over forty types of vehicle have been found by the writer listed in the toll schedules of various acts.[74]

Sometimes the tolls were levied on the horses and sometimes on the vehicles. In the example just quoted the charge is for "every horse drawing any coach". The wording might have been "for every carriage drawn by Horses". There seems at first sight no essential difference between a toll of threepence per horse and one of a shilling for a four-horsed coach, but the law-books of the period contain many records of cases

fought out in the courts on the interpretation of these terms, accompanied by the qualifying clause that tolls need not be paid on the same carriage or the same horses returning the same day.[75] Most of the cases refer to disputes over coaches repassing a gate with fresh horses or over horses returning with a different coach.

All acts contain lists of exemption, except some of the renewal acts. Exempted by the General Turnpike Acts were His Majesty's mails, military horses and

Fig. 10: Carved slate toll board showing the tolls payable at Lount Gate.

Specimen Toll Schedules

I Trent Bridge, Nottingham, to Cotes Bridge, near Loughborough (No. 3)

1st Act. 11 Geo.II, c.3 (1737-8) . . . . . . *s d*
- Coach, etc., drawn by 6 or more horses . . . 1 6
  - do.   4   do. 1 0
  - do.   3 or 2   do. 6
- Chaise, etc.,   1 horse, ... 3
- Waggon, Cart, etc. drawn by 6 horses, ... 2 0
  - do.   5 or 4   do. 1 6
  - do.   3   do. 6
  - do.   2   do. 3
  - do.   1 horse, ... 2
- Horse, etc., not drawing 1
- Cattle, etc.   per score 10
- Sheep, etc.   do. 5

2nd Act. 27 Geo.II, c.22 (1753-4)
- Tolls unchanged

3rd Act. 20 Geo.III, c.87 (1779-80)
- As above except:
- Waggon, etc., drawn by   3 horses 9
  - do.   2   do. 6
- do.   1 horse 3
- Pair of millstones 6

4th Act. 44 Geo.III, c.iv (1803-4)
- Horse, etc. drawing coach etc. 3
- do.   Waggon, etc. 4
- do.   not drawing 1
- Pair of millstones with carriage 2 6
- Cattle, sheep, etc. as in first act.

5th Act. 5 Geo.IV, c.xlvi (1824)
- As in 4th Act except that
- millstones were omitted

6th Act. 18-9 Vic., c.lxxi (1854-5)
- Horse, etc. drawing coach, waggon, etc. . . . 4
- do.   not drawing 1
- Goat drawing truck, sledge, etc. 1
- Carriage propelled by other than animal power
  - per wheel 1 0
- Cattle, sheep, etc., as above

II Bridgford Lane, Trent Bridge, Nottingham, to Melton Mowbray, Oakham, and Kettering (No. 11)

1st Act. 27 Geo.II, c.39 (1753-4) . . . . . . *s d*
- Coach, etc., drawn by   6 horses or more . 4 6
  - do.   4 horses 3 0
  - do.   3 or 2 do. . . . 2 3
- Chaise, etc. drawn by 1 horse 1 6
- Waggon, cart, etc. drawn by 4 horses or more 3 0
  - do.   3 or 2 horses . . 2 3
  - do.   1 horse 1 0
- Horse, etc., not drawing 4½
- Cattle, etc. per score 1 3
- Sheep, etc.   do. 7½

The road was divided into two districts with three gates in each and only one-third toll was to be charged at any one gate in each district.

2nd Act. 20 Geo.III, c.81 (1779-80)
- Tolls unchanged.

3rd Act. 41 Geo.III, c.cxvii (1800-1)
- Gig, etc. drawn by 1 horse, ... 6
- Horse drawing any gig, etc. with more than
- 1 horse or any coach, waggon, cart, etc. 4½

Four-wheeled vehicle fixed to another. . . .	1	6
Two- do. do. do.		9
Drug, more than 9 feet between axle trees, laden other than with 1 block of stone or timber, above the toll for the horses, ...	1	6
Horse, etc., not drawing, ...		1½

Cattle, etc.,	per score,	. . . .	10
Sheep, etc.,	do.	. . . . .	5

Only one toll a day between Trent Bridge and Leicestershire boundary; two tolls a day thence to Oakham; three tolls a day thence to Kettering.

4th Act. 4 Geo.IV, c.lvi. (1823)
Tolls unchanged.

III The Moira and Gresley Roads (No. 30)

1st Act. 34 Geo.III, c.120 (1794) . . . . . . *s d*
Horse, etc. drawing any coach, waggon, etc.
gates from Caddow Gate to the
Burton-Ashby rd, ... 4½
any other gate 2½
Horse, etc., not drawing 1
Cattle, etc., per score 10
Sheep, etc., do. 5

2nd Act. 55 Geo.III, c.lxiii (1815)
Horse drawing any coach, waggon, etc. 6

Horse not drawing 1
Cattle, sheep, etc., as above

3rd Act. 4-5 Wm.IV, c.lx (1834)
As above with addition of
Any carriage propelled by steam etc. 5 0

4th Act. 27-8 Vic., c.lxx (1864)
Horse drawing any coach, waggon, etc. 4
Horse not drawing 1
Cattle, sheep, etc., as above

IV Measham to Fieldon Bridge, etc. (No. 19B)

1 Wm. IV, c.xii (1830-1) . . . . . . *s d*
Horse drawing any coach, etc. 4½
do. waggon, etc., wheels 6 ins or more . 4
do. do. do. 4 ½ to 6 ins . . 5
do. do. do. less than 4 ½ ins 6
Horse not drawing 1½

Cattle, etc. per score 1 3
Sheep, etc. do. 7
Millstones per pair 2 6
Coach, waggon, etc., propelled by steam or gas 2 6
Cart drawn by 1 horse only, for every cwt.
above 1½ tons, in addition to above. 3

V Coventry to Stoney Stanton (No. 34)

1 Wm.IV, c.xl (1830-1) . . . . . . *s d*
As for Measham to Fieldon Bridge,
except: first item 3
cattle per score. 10
sheep do. 5

VI Watling Street, etc. (No.22A)

1 Wm.IV, c.xiv (1830-31)
As for Measham to Fieldon Bridge.

waggons, carriages of persons going to church or to elections, beasts going to water, etc. Local exemptions were varied in the extreme. There were clauses freeing from tolls certain articles of commerce, certain persons and inhabitants of particular villages. The Nottingham to Kettering Act of 1753-4 exempted all the residents of certain villages in the Vale of Belvoir and near it from toll at Melton Mowbray gate.[76] This was due to the fact that such people, going to Melton, need not join the main road until nearly in the town and only used a few yards of it. To facilitate the operation of this exemption clause, the surveyor of highways of each of the villages had to provide the toll collector with lists of inhabitants annually.

Fig. 11: The Dane Hill toll bar for the Hinckley Road on the outskirts of Leicester.

List of Villages whose Inhabitants were Exempt from Toll at the Spittle End of Toll Gate, Melton Mowbray, by the Nottingham to Kettering Act of 1753-4 27 Geo.II, c.39

(a) Holwell	(a) Hose	(a) Harby
Long Clawson	(a) Stathern	(a) Eastwell
Asfordby	Saxelby	(a) Plungar
(a) Barkston	(a) Redmile	(a) Bottesford
(a) Normanton	Grimston	Shoby
Ragdale	Hoby	Thrussington
(a) Easthorp	Cossington	(a) Muston
Dalby on the Wolds	Prestwold	Walton on the Wolds
Sileby	Loughborough	Ratcliffe on the Wreak
Quorn	Mount Sorrel	
Seagrave	Wymeswold	Barrow on Soar
Willoughby	Burton by Loughborough	

The villages marked (a) were omitted from the list in the renewal Act of 1779-80 – 20 Geo.III, c.81

There was a reciprocal arrangement by which Melton residents were exempt at the same gate while on journeys to any listed places.

Finance

No trust could expect to gather much at the tollgates until a start at least had been made on getting the roads in order, and nothing at all before the gates themselves and the collectors' houses that went with them were erected. Each trust therefore began its existence with a loan and, theoretically, when the trust was a going concern, the takings at the gates should have been sufficient to cover salaries and wages, upkeep of the roads, improvements such as the lowering of hills, interest on loans and gradual repayment of principal.

A trust was not a commercial company. The road was still a public highway and the trustees were public commissioners, who, as trustees, made no profit and earned no dividend.[77] Individual trustees could lend money to the trust and receive fixed interest and loans could also be raised from outside people.

The early acts contained clauses stipulating that the roads should be freed from toll when certificates of the justices could be produced to the effect that the roads were put in order. Rarely, if ever, did these clauses operate, for when an act expired, usually after 21 years, it was necessary to seek renewal (at, by the way, huge legal cost) by petition to Parliament and in order that time be given for repayment of loans, even if the roads were repaired and needed little beyond the statute labour of maintenance. Often there were not only loans to repay, but arrears of interest as well, sometimes equalling in amount the principal debt or even exceeding it. As time went on and traffic increased, maintenance costs grew, and it was only trustees of the best patronised and best managed roads that could remain solvent.

When the "calamity of railways" occurred and toll receipts began to decline, many trusts found themselves in financial straits with large debts, many years of unpaid interest, and no hope of recovery even by increased tolls. At the same time as railways were beginning to spread, the General Turnpike Act of 1835 abolished statute labour.[78]

In 1831, with two objects in view, Parliament passed the first of what grew to be a long series of Annual Turnpike Trusts Continuance Acts.[79] One of the objects was the saving of parliamentary time. The other was the facilitating of road development by

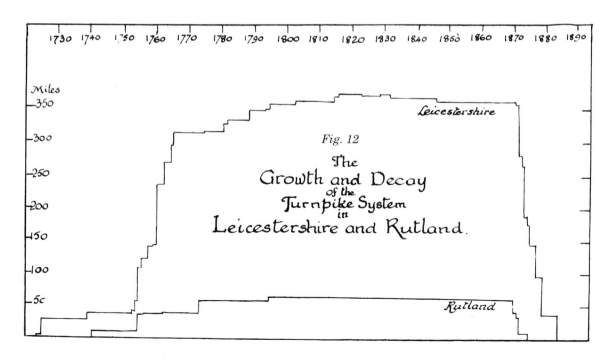

Fig. 12

The Growth and Decay of the Turnpike System in Leicestershire and Rutland.

Toll Bridges

Bridges for the crossing of which tolls were charged were in a different category from turnpike roads. As stated on page 25, turnpike trustees could lend money to trusts and receive interest, but there was no dividend.

A toll bridge was usually built under powers of a special Act of Parliament which appointed trustees to issue shares, or which gave powers to build to a private person. Profits made from the tolls were divided among the shareholders or drawn by the individual owner.

The bridges that replaced Wilne and Sawley Ferries over the Trent in the north-western corner of Leicestershire were toll bridges. On petition of the High Sheriff, justices and other influential persons of Derbyshire, powers were gained by the Act 31 Geo.II, c.59 (1757-8) for the replacement of Wilne Ferry by the bridge that became known as Cavendish Bridge. The Act received Royal Assent on 9 June 1758. The bridge was opened in 1771. By the Act the trustees had to pay £150 a year to the Lord of the Manor of Castle Donington (then Sir Matthew Lamb) and £3. 6s.8d. a year to the field reeves or other parish officers of Castle Donington for the use of the parish. It seems that Cavendish Bridge became a paying concern for the rent charges were redeemed in about fifty years and the bridge freed from toll in 1817. The trustees still managed the bridge and, as will be seen later, must have had a considerable fund in hand.

A petition by Charles, Earl of Harrington, later resulted in the Act 28 Geo.III, c.80, receiving the Royal Assent on 11 June 1788, for the replacement of Sawley Ferry by what was known as the Harrington Bridge. In this case, the rent charges were £50 a year to the Earl and £1 a year to Sir Henry Harpur. After paying dividend on the shares (£50 each) at a rate not to exceed 7 per cent, half the residue was to go to the Earl, provided that his total income from the bridge did not exceed £100. Any further residue was to be used for redemption of the shares. According to Bagshaw, the first stone of the bridge was laid in 1786 and the bridge opened in 1789.[80] A first bridge, says the same authority, was swept away by floods before completion. The discrepancies in dates seem to point to the 1786 event being in respect of the first bridge and that it was started without parliamentary authority. If it were the second bridge, it must have been commenced in anticipation of the Act being passed.

Fig. 13: Scale of toll charges for Cavendish Bridge over the Trent on the Leicestershire-Derbyshire border, "being the same that were taken at the Ferry".

When railways came in the toll receipts dropped and from 1839 onwards there was insufficient money to pay the 7 per cent dividend. In 1880 and 1881 the dividend was only ¾ per cent. In 1882 shares to the nominal value of £5,940 were still unredeemed.

In that year, by the Act 45-6 Vic., c.xxi, the Harrington Bridge was handed over to the Cavendish Bridge trustees, £1,500 paid to the Earl of Harrington and £25 to the representative of the Harpur interest. The shareholders divided £1,420 13s. Tolls were then suspended, although a private proviso was inserted in the Act authorising their temporary levying in case extraordinary repairs should be necessary.

In 1896, by 59-60 Vic., c.xix, the bridges were taken over by the then new County Councils, that at Sawley going to Derbyshire and Cavendish Bridge going to Leicestershire. Money still in the trustees' hands was used for the building of Borrowash Bridge, near Derby. The Harrington Bridge was considerably altered soon afterwards, but parts of the old bridge remain.

Old Cavendish Bridge is now no more. A splendid example of the work of the eighteenth century civil engineers, it remained unspoiled by such ugly "improvements" as footpaths on brackets, to the end, which came suddenly in 1947 when it was swept away by the great floods in March. It is true that to modern road traffic the bridge was an impediment. It was narrow, rather hump-backed, and its approaches, especially on the Leicestershire side, were awkward to negotiate. Hopes that modernization of the crossing would involve a new bridge without destruction of the old have now alas! to be abandoned. The toll house still stands, although it may have to give way for the new bridge. It bears on its front a slate tablet with the list of tolls that were charged. These were very similar to those charged at turnpike gates: half a crown for a four-wheeled carriage, a shilling for a two-wheeled chaise, etc., eighteen pence for a four-wheeled waggon, a shilling for a two-wheeled cart, a penny for a horse not drawing, sixpence a score for pigs, fourpence a score for sheep, a halfpenny a head for cattle and – here a toll bridge schedule always differed from that of a turnpike road – a penny for a foot passenger. A final item reads, "Soldiers (favour'd) each…0.0½ d." It does not appear whether this means that soldiers were a favoured class or that the lower rate was for enlisted men wearing favours.

Fig. 14: The old Cavendish Bridge, opened as a toll bridge in 1771, was washed away by floods in 1947

relieving the trusts of the costs attendant upon the passing of renewal acts. By this Act and its successors, all local turnpike acts due to expire were continued for a year automatically and, unless the trustees desired alterations of their powers or extensions of routes, there was no need for a separate local act. When the railways showed that they had come to stay and the traffic on the roads more and more rapidly decreased, it was by means of these annual acts that the turnpike system was abolished. Exceptions began to creep into the annual acts. Later, schedules were added listing trusts that were not continued beyond certain dates, others to be continued with modifications of their financial arrangements and others to continue "unless Parliament otherwise provides". The schedules gradually increased in length and by the 1870s disturnpiking was in full swing. Few trusts lived beyond the middle 1880s.

Meanwhile in order to better the financial position of trusts whose local acts were not due for renewal and therefore not yet affected by the Continuance Acts, power was given for trustees to seek Provisional Orders from the Secretary of State enabling them to reduce interest and perhaps extinguish arrears.[81] To confirm these Provisional Orders, another series of acts was commenced, the Annual Turnpike Trusts Arrangements Acts.

The following statistics for England and Wales show that at the time of the introduction of railways, toll receipts were on the increase, but a rapid fall had already set in by 1849, accompanied by a heavy rise in the amount of unpaid interest.[82]

TURNPIKE TRUST.

Expiration of the Local Act of Parliament and Sale of the Toll Houses and Gates.

NOTICE IS HEREBY GIVEN

That in consequence of the Abolition of the Tolls on this Road on the 1st day of November, 1880, the

MATERIALS OF THE TOLL HOUSES

AND THE TURNPIKE GATES,

WILL BE SOLD BY PUBLIC AUCTION,

For removal immediately after that day, by

MESSRS. GERMAN, GERMAN, AND LOWE,

Subject to such Conditions as will be read at the Time of Sale, and at the following times and places:

LOT 1.—THE HINCKLEY GATE TOLL HOUSE and Gate, on Thursday, the 28th day of October, 1880, at 11 o'clock in the Forenoon precisely, at the Hinckley Gate.

LOT 2.—THE STAPLETON GATE TOLL HOUSE and Gate, on the same day, at 11.30 o'clock in the Forenoon precisely, at the Stapleton Gate.

LOT 3.—THE CADEBY MACHINE GATE TOLL HOUSE and Gate, on the same day, at 12 o'clock in the Afternoon precisely, at the Cadeby Machine Gate.

LOT 4.—THE OSBASTON BAR TOLL HOUSE and Gate, on the same day, at 12.30 o'clock in the Afternoon precisely, at the Osbaston Bar.

LOT 5.—THE OSBASTON GATE TOLL HOUSE and Gate, on the same day at 12.45 o'clock in the Afternoon precisely at the Osbaston Gate Toll House.

LOT 6.—THE BELCHER'S BAR TOLL HOUSE and Gate, on the same day, at 3 o'clock in the Afternoon precisely, at the Belcher's Bar.

LOT 7.—THE PISCA LANE BAR TOLL HOUSE and Gate, on the same day, at 3.30 o'clock in the Afternoon, at Pisca Lane Bar.

LOT 8.—THE HEATHER MILL BAR TOLL HOUSE and Bar, on the same day at 4 o'clock in the Afternoon precisely, at the Heather Mill Bar.

LOT 9.—THE SWEPSTONE BAR TOLL HOUSE and Bar, on the same day, at 4.30 o'clock in the Afternoon precisely, at the Swepstone Bar.

LOT 10.—THE OLD LANE GATE TOLL HOUSE and Gate, on Friday, the 29th day of October, 1880, at 10.30 o'clock in the Forenoon precisely, at the Old Lane Gate.

LOT 11.—THE SWANNINGTON BAR TOLL HOUSE and Gate, on the same day, at 11 o'clock in the Forenoon at Swannington Bar.

LOT 12.—THE FROGGATT'S LANE TOLL HOUSE and Gate, on the same day at 11.30 o'clock in the Forenoon precisely, at the Froggatt's Lane Gate.

LOT 13.—THE FROGGATT'S LANE BAR TOLL HOUSE and Bar on the same day at 11.45 o'clock in the Forenoon precisely, at the Froggatt's Lane Bar.

LOT 14.—THE CLOUDWOOD BAR TOLL HUT and Bar, on the same day, at 12.30 o'clock in the Afternoon precisely, at the Cloudwood Bar.

LOT 15.—THE REDWOOD GATE TOLL HOUSE and Gate, on the same day at 12.39 o'clock in the Afternoon precisely, at the Redwood Gate.

LOT 16.—THE ENGINE GATE TOLL HOUSE and Gate, on the same day, at 2 o'clock in the Afternoon precisely, at the Engine Gate.

LOT 17.—THE CARTBROOK BAR TOLL HOUSE and Bar, on the same day, at 2.30 o'clock in the Afternoon precisely, at the Cartbrook Bar.

Fig. 15: Notice of sale of the toll houses and gates of the Hinckley to Woeful Bridge and Measham turnpike (No. 18) in 1880.

Turnpike Finances: England and Wales

	Toll receipts	Total income:
1834	£1,431,609	?
1837	?	£1,699,428
1839	£1.532,956	?
1849	?	£1,177,981

	Mortgage Debt:	Unpaid interest:
1834	£7,068,275	£1,002,255
1837	£7,011,989	£1,019,568
1839	£7,238,935	£1,194,699
1849	£6,382.647	£1,587,010

The year 1837 was the peak year for toll receipts and, although the 1839 figures show an increase over 1834, the decline had already set in in some parts of the country. The decrease was most marked in the counties through which the London to Birmingham railway passed. The following are a selection of county figures.

Toll receipts		
	1834	**1849**
Leicester	£24,381	£24,903
Rutland	£3,757	£3,670
Derby	£31,084	£38,258
Warwick	£26,785	£27,728
Northampton	£32,424	£30,847
Buckingham	£18,554	£13,875
Bedford	£12,689	£10,649
Middlesex	£91,760	£81,470
Norfolk	£9,797	£14,390
Devon	£49,398	£54,545
Hereford	£15,013	£20,932
Nottingham	£16,218	£16,255
Hertford	£26,601	£25,617
England and Wales	£1,431,609	£1,532,956

Fig. 16: Petition of 1872 by the Snareston parish authorities for the removal of the now defunct toll gate house from its location "only ten feet from the centre of the road", to ensure they could reclaim "their proper width of highway."

Particularly to be noticed are the decreases in Middlesex, Hertford, Bedford, Buckingham and Northampton through which the Birmingham railway passed, and the increases in such counties far from the early railways as Devon, Hereford and especially Norfolk.

For comparison with the above toll receipts, the following figures for rates levied for the upkeep of highways other than turnpikes should be noticed, together with the mileage covered by both types of administration. These amounts are for the year ending 25 March 1839.

At this period the ratio of mileage of turnpike road to total length of all roads was

	per cent
England and Wales	13.5
Leicester	15.9
Rutland	18.3
Derby	25.3
Warwick	17.2
Nottingham	17.5
Northampton	17.5
Norfolk	7.3
Suffolk	6.5

Mileage [83]			**Highway**
Under Street Commissioners	Turnpike Trusts	Other	**Rates**
Leics	31	302	1,558	£23,021
Rutland	—	57	253	£4,148

Notes on the County Maps over the following pages

The county maps showing the development of the turnpike system in Leicestershire and Rutland have been chosen for 1750, when only the great through routes were turnpiked; 1755, when the coalfield was first reached, by the Leicester to Ashby and Burton roads; 1760, to show the intensification of turnpiking on the coalfield; and at two 40-year intervals, 1800 and 1840, to show the slow development after the coalfield roads had been included in the system. Two maps show the process of disturnpiking, one for 1875 and the other for 1880. A map for the end of 1885 would show the last turnpiked road gone.

The road numbering on the county maps corresponds to that in the Gazetteer, where each individual route has also reproduced. To minimise crowding, the road numbers are not repeated on subsequent maps, unless branches were added.

The county map showing the Royal Mail routes (fig. 24) does not include the cross routes. There were a few mail coaches running on branch roads but it is difficult to map them as it is possible that they did not go direct from the nearest London mail stage but "wandered" to serve places off the road. There were also cross mails not carried by coach.

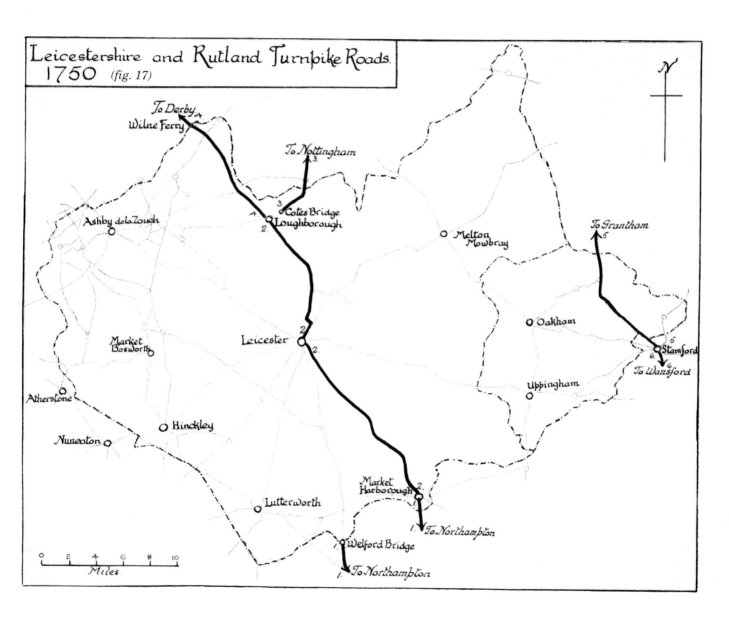

Leicestershire and Rutland Turnpike Roads.
1750 (fig. 17)

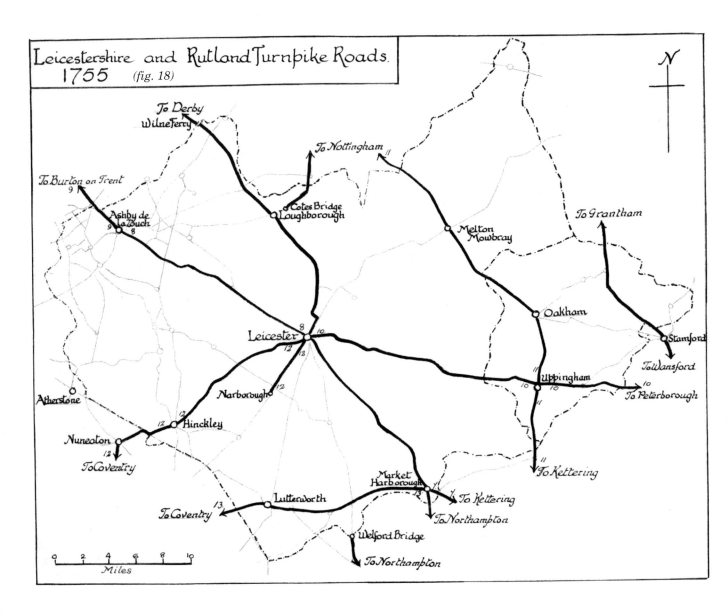

Leicestershire and Rutland Turnpike Roads. 1755 (fig. 18)

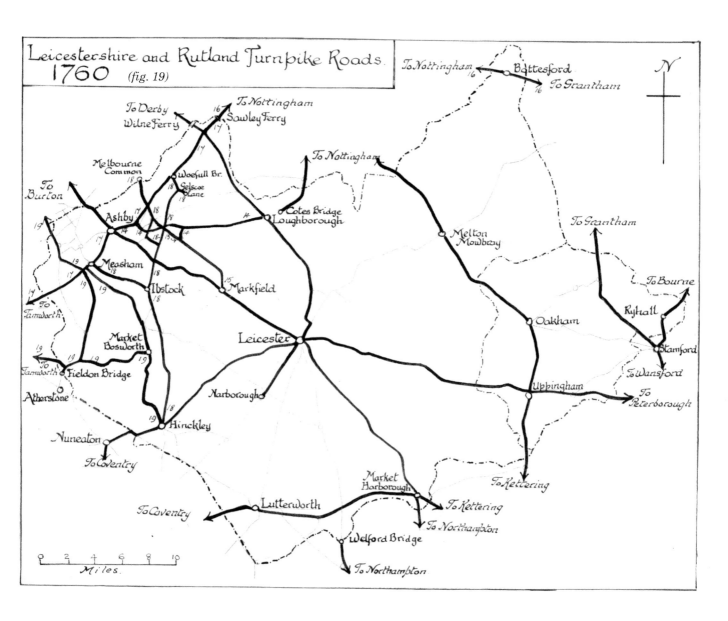

Leicestershire and Rutland Turnpike Roads.
1760 (fig. 19)

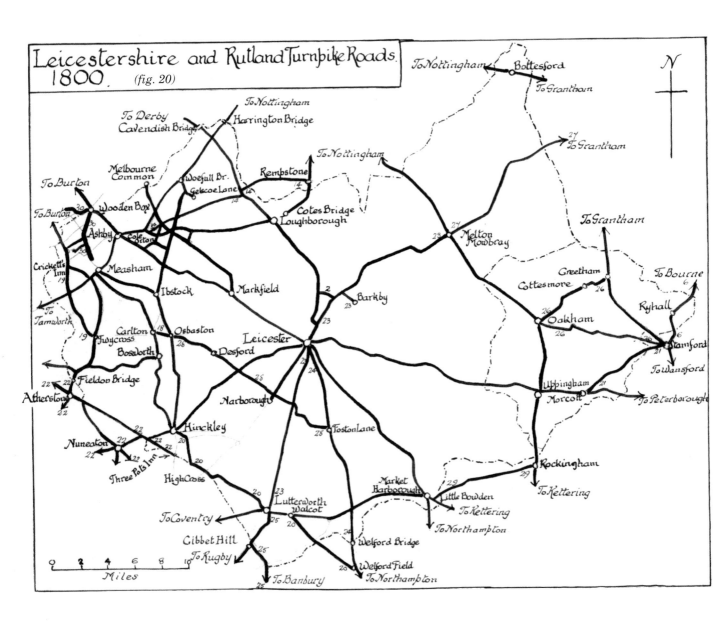

Leicestershire and Rutland Turnpike Roads. 1800. *(fig. 20)*

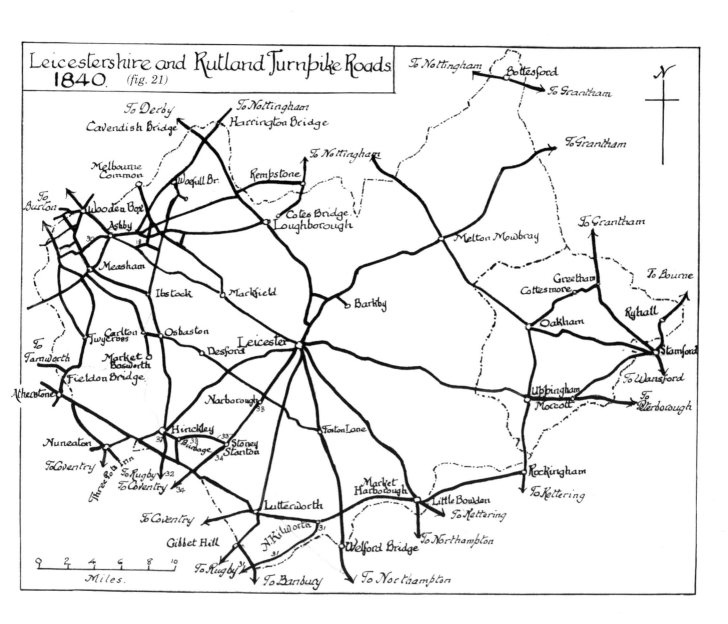

Leicestershire and Rutland Turnpike Roads. 1840. *(fig. 21)*

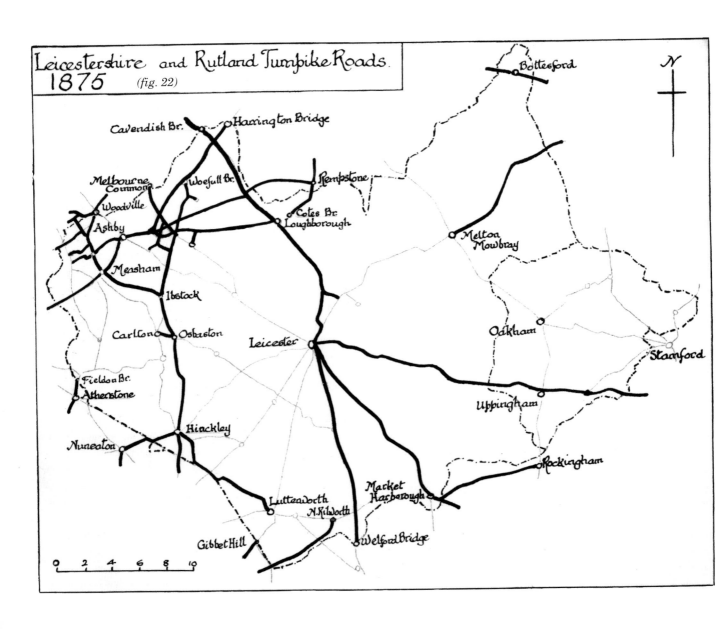

Leicestershire and Rutland Turnpike Roads. 1875 *(fig. 22)*

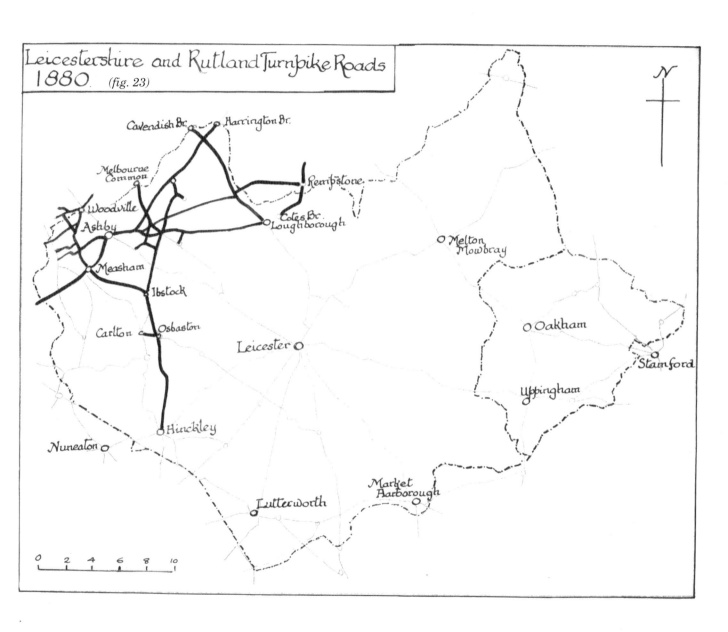

Leicestershire and Rutland Turnpike Roads 1880. *(fig. 23)*

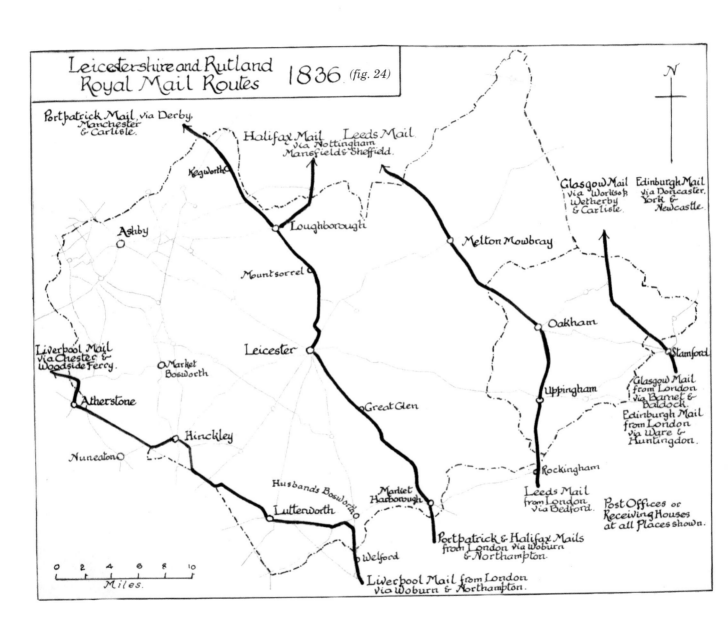

Leicestershire and Rutland Royal Mail Routes 1836 *(fig. 24)*

N

Portpatrick Mail, via Derby, Manchester & Carlisle.

Halifax Mail via Nottingham Mansfield & Sheffield.

Leeds Mail

Kegworth

Ashby

Loughborough

Mountsorrel

Leicester

O Market Bosworth

Melton Mowbray

Glasgow Mail via Worksop Wetherby & Carlisle.

Edinburgh Mail via Doncaster York & Newcastle.

Oakham

Stamford

Liverpool Mail via Chester & Woodside Ferry.

Atherstone

Hinckley

Nuneaton O

Great Glen

Uppingham

Glasgow Mail from London via Barnet & Baldock.

Edinburgh Mail from London via Ware & Huntingdon.

Husband's Bosworth

Market Harborough

Rockingham

Lutterworth

Leeds Mail from London via Bedford.

Post Offices or Receiving Houses at all Places shown.

Welford

Portpatrick & Halifax Mails from London via Woburn & Northampton.

Liverpool Mail from London via Woburn & Northampton.

0 2 4 6 8 10
Miles.

GAZETTEER

A Chronological List of the Turnpike Roads of Leicestershire and Rutland, with the Acts under which they were Operated

Abbreviations used in the gazetteer

Act of 1st Auth.	Act by which the road was first authorised to be turnpiked.
Cont. Act	Continuation Act, extending operation for further term, usually with altered powers.
Amend. Act	Amending Act.
Re-enact.	Act for repeal of the previous Acts still in force, and for re-enactment.
Cont. Act (Section)	Continuation Act for a section of road only.
Re-enact. (Section)	Repeal and re-enactment for section only.
Revival	Revival of lapsed authorisation.
Ann. Cont. Act	Annual Continuance Act.
Prov. Order	Provisional Order.
ATTA Act	Annual Turnpike Trusts Arrangements Act, confirming Provisional Order.
Sched.	Scheduled.
Mod.	Modifications of financial powers.
HCJ	House of Commons Journal.
To expire	The date at which the powers of the trustees were to expire.
Repealed	An act or provision to end the turnpiking powers of a trust.

The numbers of the roads are those of the County Maps on pages 31 to 37.

Where applicable, 'A road' numbers are also given. Many of the turnpike routes went on to become 'A roads' under the 1919 Ministry of Transport Act, Section 17(2).[84] These routes remained largely unchanged until the road building programmes of the late twentieth century.

Note on the numbering of Acts of Parliament

Up to and including the session 1796-7 (37 Geo.III), there were two series of Acts:

i   Public Acts, numbered in Arabic numerals, e.g. 3 Geo.I, c.4
ii Private Acts, similarly numbered, e.g. 3 Geo.I, c.4 Pr

From 38 Geo.III onwards, there were three series:

i   Public General Acts, numbered in Arabic numerals e.g. 42 Geo.III, c.12
ii Public Local Acts, numbered in small Roman numerals, e.g. 42 Geo.III, c.xii
iii Private Acts, numbered in Arabic numerals, e.g. 42 Geo.III, c.12 Pr

Turnpike Acts, except for a few very early ones, were in the Public Local Category and thus were in group i before 1798 and group ii afterwards. For a few years before 1798 however they were described as 'Public Acts known as Road Acts', but, being numbered consecutively with the other Public Acts, this makes no difference to their citation. The Annual Continuance Acts and the Annual Turnpike Trusts Arrangements Acts were Public General Acts except, for some unknown reason, the Continuance Act of 1875, which was Local and cited as 38-9 Vic., c.cxciv

1

Brampton Bridge, Church Brampton, Northants, to Welford Bridge; Mortar Pit Hill to Chain Bridge, Market Harborough

(later became the A50 and A508)

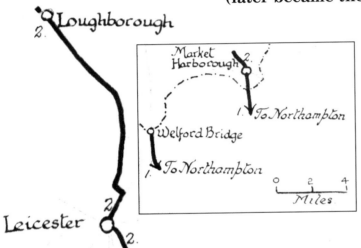

1721-2	Act of 1st Auth.	8 Geo.I, c.13
1738-9	Cont. Act	12 Geo.II, c.35
	Both branches extended southward to Kingsthorpe, Northampton.	
1749-50	Cont. Act	23 Geo.II, c.8
1777-8	Re-enact.	18 Geo.III, c.112
1810	Re-enact.	50 Geo.III, c.cliv
1822	Re-enact.	3 Geo.IV, c.c
1867-8	Ann. Cont. Act	31-2 Vic., c 99
	(Sched. out of debt)	
1870	Ann. Cont. Act	33-4 Vic., c.73
	(Sched. out of debt)	
1872	Ann. Cont. Act	35-6 Vic., c.85
	(**To expire:** 1 Nov. 1872)	

2

'The London to Manchester Road'
Market Harborough to Loughborough

(later became the A6)

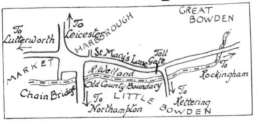

Fig. 25: Streets and road routes through Market Harborough showing the pre-1888 county boundary.

1725-6	Act of 1st Auth.	12 Geo.I, c.5
1745-6	Cont. Act	19 Geo.II, c.10

With branch: Filling Gate to the Fosse Way and the Melton Mowbray road, via Wanlip.

1770-1	Cont. Act	11 Geo.III, c.88
1792-3	Cont. Act	33 Geo.III, c.176

1812-3	**Cont. Act**	53 Geo.III, c.xxiii
1830	**Re-enact.**	11 Geo.IV and 1 Wm.IV, c.iii
Branch omitted		
1863	**Re-enact.**	26-7 Vic., c.iv
1878	**Ann. Cont. Act**	41-2 Vic., c.62
(Repealed: 1 Nov. 1878))		

By the 1863 Act no tolls were to be taken or money spent on the road in Leicester itself, defined as between the junction of Occupation Road with London Road and the junction between the main road and Sidney Street. A full history of this road is contained in *A Leicestershire Road,* by Percy Russell, (Leicester, Backus, 1934).

3

Trent Bridge, Nottingham, to Cotes Bridge, via Bunny and Rempstone
(later became the A60)

1737-8	**Act of 1st Auth.**	11 Geo.II, c.3
1753-4	**Cont. Act**	27 Geo.II, c.22
1779-80	**Re-enact.**	20 Geo.III, c.87
1803-4	**Cont. Act**	44 Geo.III, c.iv
1824	**Re-enact.**	5 Geo.IV, c.xlvi
1854-5	**Re-enact.**	18-19 Vic., c.lxxi
1877	**Ann. Cont. Act**	40-1 Vic., c.64

(Mod. from 1 Nov.1877: no interest payable; repairs not to be less than £200 p.a.
To expire: 1 Nov. 1880)

A previous petition, prepared in 1732, sought to make into a turnpike road the route from Nottingham to Loughborough, via Bunny, Stanford on Soar and Loughborough Town Meadow. (MS. Notts. Q.S.Minute Book, 15 Feb. 1732). No entry appears in the HCJ regarding this petition. It was apparently never presented.

Prior to the passing of the Act of 1779-80, a petition asked for the inclusion of the continuation of the road from Cotes Bridge to London Road, Loughborough. Power was given to the Committee to make provision for this extension (HCJ 2 and 7 March 1780). No further entry, however, occurs.

For a description of this road as it was in 1796, extracted from Marshall's *Rural Economy of the Midland Counties,* see page 9 .

The diversion on Wilford Hill, near Nottingham, was made in 1805, as appears by an advertisement in the Nottingham Journal for 21 December in that year, announcing the holding of a meeting of the trustees to make an exchange with the owner of the land, Sir Gervase Clifton, who had lately allowed the diversion on his property.

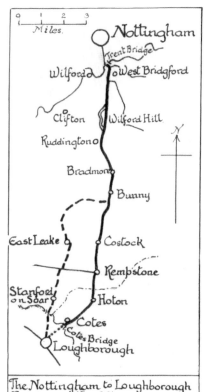

The Nottingham to Loughborough Road. *(fig. 26)*

4

'The London to Manchester Road'
Loughborough to Derby, via Wilne Ferry; Derby to Brassington; Derby to Hurdloe via Ashbourne
(sections later became the A6)

1737-8	**Act of 1st Auth.**	11 Geo.II, c.33
1743-4	**Cont. Act**	17 Geo.II, c.20
1759-60	**Cont. Act**	33 Geo.II, c.33

4.A (Part of above) **South-east end of Loughborough to Derby Bridge, near the Rushes, Loughborough, and thence to Cavendish Bridge.**

1776-7	**Re-enact. (Section)**	17 Geo.III, c.108
1807	**Revival**	47 Geo.III, sess. 2 c. xix
1826-7	**Re-enact.**	7-8 Geo.IV, c.lxxiv
1830-1	**Re-enact.**	1 Wm.IV, c.lxvii
1866, 10 July	Amalgamated with No.14	
1884	**Ann. Cont. Act**	47-8 Vic., c.52

(United roads **Repealed**: 25 Mar. 1885)

Cavendish Bridge succeeded Wilne or Wilden Ferry. See Box on pages 26-27.

The Derbyshire portions of the original road were administered under separate series of Acts from 17 Geo.III onwards, as follows:

Gaol Bridge, Derby, to Hurdloe House, via Ashbourne.

1776-7	**Re-enact. (Section)**	17 Geo.III, c.92
1805	**Cont. Act**	45 Geo.III, c.i
1828	**Re-enact.**	9 Geo.IV, c.lxxix
1851	**Re-enact.**	14-15 Vic., c.xxxiv
1873	**Ann. Cont. Act**	36-7 Vic., c.90

(North Divn. **To expire:** 1 Nov. 1873.)
(South Divn. Mod. From 1 Nov. 1873: tolls reduced by one third; salaries and law charges limited to £75 p.a.; no interest payable; **To expire:** 1 Nov. 1875.)

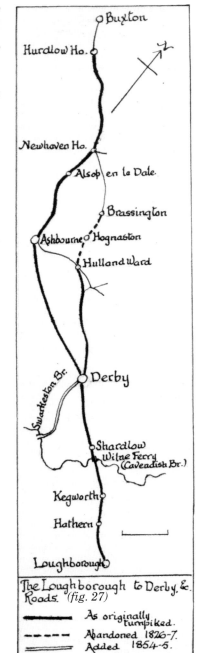

The Loughborough to Derby, & Roads. (fig. 27)

▬▬▬ As originally turnpiked.
- - - - - Abandoned 1826-7.
═══ Added 1854-5.

Cavendish Bridge, via Derby, to Brassington.

| 1776-7 | **Re-enact. (Section)** | 17 Geo.III, c.101 |
| 1806 | **Cont. Act** | 46 Geo.III, c.xcviii |

Hulland Ward to Brassington abandoned

| 1826-7 | **Re-enact.** | 7-8 Geo.IV, c.1 |

With addition of Derby to Swarkeston Bridge.

| 1854-5 | **Re-enact.** | 18-19 Vic., c.clxviii |
| 1877 | **Ann. Cont. Act** | 40-1 Vic., c.64 |

(Mod. from 1 Nov. 1877: no interest payable; **To expire:** 1 Nov. 1879)

5

'The Great North Road'
Stamford to Grantham
(later became the A1)

1738-9	**Act of 1st Auth.**	12 Geo.II, c.8
1750-1	**Cont. Act**	24 Geo.II, c.3
1787	**Cont. Act**	27 Geo.II, c.92

5.A South Division of the above: Stamford to the Division Stone, South Witham.

1808	**Re-enact. (Section)**	48 Geo.III, c.cxiii
1830	**Re-enact.**	11 Geo.IV & 1 Wm.IV, c.xciii
1873	**Ann. Cont. Act**	36-7 Vic., c.90

(**To expire:** 31 Dec. 1873)

The remainder of this road, from South Witham to Grantham, was amalgamated with the road from Grantham to Foston Bridge, which was separated from the Grantham to Little Drayton (Nottinghamshire) trust. The sections in Lincolnshire and Nottinghamshire were administered under the following Acts:

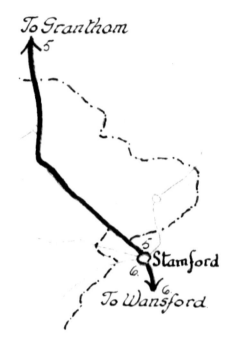

Grantham to Little Drayton

| 1725-6 | **Act of 1st Auth.** | 12 Geo.I, c.16 |
| 1738-9 | **Cont. Act** | 12 Geo.II, c.34 |

Foston Bridge to Little Drayton.

1766-7	**Cont. Act (Section)**	7 Geo.III, c.78
1798-9	**Re-enact.**	39 Geo.III, c.xxvi
1821	**Re-enact.**	1-2 Geo.IV, c.xxix
1821	**Amend. Act**	1-2 Geo.IV, c.xcv
1872	**Ann. Cont. Act**	35-6 Vic., c.85

(**To expire:** 1 Nov. 1872)

Grantham to Foston Bridge.

| 1765-6 | **Cont. Act (Section)** | 6 Geo.III, c.83 |
| 1786 | **Cont. Act** | 26 Geo.III, c.138 |

Amalgamated with South Witham to Grantham (North Division of Stamford to Grantham No. 5):

South Witham to Foston Bridge.

1808	**Re-enact. (Section)**	48 Geo.III, c.lxiii
1830	**Re-enact.**	11 Geo.IV & 1 Wm.IV, c.xc
1867-8	**Ann. Cont. Act**	31-2 Vic., c.99
	(Sched. out of debt)	
1870	**Ann. Cont. Act**	33-4 Vic., c.73
	(To expire: 1 Nov. 1870)	

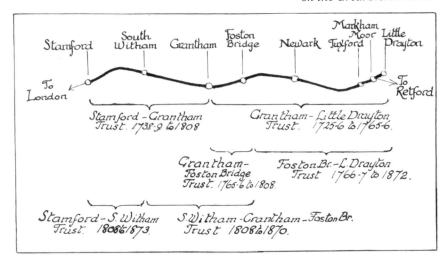

Fig. 28: Turnpike trust amalgamations on the Great North Road.

6

'The Great North Road'
Wansford to Stamford Bridge
(later became the A1)

1748-9	**Act of 1st Auth.**	22 Geo.II, c.17

With addition of Stamford to Bourne, via Ryhall.

1755-6	**Cont. Act**	29 Geo.II, c.76

With addition of (i) North end of Stamford Bridge to Scot Gate, Stamford, and (ii) former terminus in Bourne to Market Cross, Bourne.

1775-6	**Cont. Act**	16 Geo.III, c.74

1797-8	**Cont. Act**	38 Geo.III, c.xlix
1820	**Re-enact.**	1 Geo.IV, c.xxii
1823	**Re-enact.**	4 Geo.IV, c.cxi
1871	**Ann. Cont. Act**	34-5 Vic., c.115
	(To expire: 1 Nov. 1871)	

A very short section of this road is in Rutland, the remainder being in Lincolnshire and Northamptonshire

7

'The London to Manchester Road'
Market Harborough to Kettering and the Pound, Brampton, Huntingdonshire
(later became the A6)

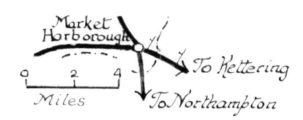

1751-2	**Act of 1st Auth.**	25 Geo.II, c.57
1753-4	**Amend. Act**	27 Geo.II, c.28
1759-60	**Cont. Act**	33 Geo.II, c.38
1798-9	**Cont. Act**	39 Geo.III, c.1
1820	**Cont. Act**	1 Geo.IV, c.lxxx
1841	**Re-enact.**	4-5 Vic., c.xxxv
1842	**Amend. Act**	5-6 Vic., c.lxix
1873	**Ann. Cont. Act**	36-7 Vic., c.90

(Mod. from 1 Nov. 1873: no expenditure on repairs between Market Harborough and St. Mary's Bridge; salaries, law charges and incidentals limited to £50 p.a.; **To expire:** 1 Nov. 1877)

Before the boundary extension, under the Local Government Act of 1888, brought Little Bowden into Leicestershire, the whole of this road was in Northamptonshire and Huntingdonshire, except for the short stretch between Market Harborough and the Welland.

The Market Harborough to Kettering section had been included in an abortive scheme two years earlier. Petitions for the turnpiking of the road from Westwood Gate, Bedfordshire, to Market Harborough, via Kettering, were presented to Parliament in 1749, at the same time as others were being presented for the renewal of the Northampton to Market Harborough and Welford Acts (No.1). The two routes were, of course, alternative ways from London to the North.

The Kettering route was favoured by petitioners from Bedfordshire to Northamptonshire (18 Dec.), Kettering (25 Jan.), Sheffield, Chesterfield, Leicester and Market Harborough (29 Jan.) The bill was read a second time on 29 Jan. and sent to a committee after a division, 197 to 186. On the same day a petition against the Kettering route from the Rev. Stephen Langton of Cottesbrook, who had lent money to the Northampton trust, was presented. Petitions for the Kettering route continued to arrive: from Nottingham and Derby (31 Jan.), Luton (1 Feb.) and Mansfield (5 Feb.). The bill was reported on 13 February, but the motion for engrossing it was lost, 208 to 154. The Northampton renewal bill was passed. (HCJ, 23 Geo.II relevant dates).

The amending Act of 27 Geo.II was due to the following circumstances. The trustees had diverted the pre-turnpike exit from Market Harborough and doubted the legality of their action. The old road to Kettering led over the Chain Bridge and through the tollgate of the Northampton trust into Little Bowden. The diversion obviated interference with the Northampton trust's territory by passing through St. Mary's Lane and along part of the road leading to St. Mary's Bridge. This road, apparently, had not been a public road, so the amending Act declared it one and authorised the erection of a tollgate upon it. See figure 25 on page 40.

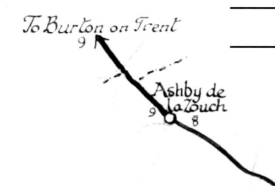

8

Leicester to Ashby de la Zouch
(later became the A50)

By the 1842 Act the termini were defined as: Leicester, the Woodgate, 100 yards north of the North Bridge; Ashby, 88 yards east of the south-west corner of the house of John Eames. Kelly's Directory of 1849 gives a Mr John Eames living in Upper Church Street, Ashby.

1753	**Act of 1st Auth.**	26 Geo.II, c.46
(1753-4	**Amend. Act**	27 Geo.II, c.42)
1778-9	**Cont. Act**	19 Geo.III, c.90
1799-1800	**Cont. Act**	39-40 Geo.III, c.ii
1821	**Cont. Act**	1-2 Geo.IV, c.viii
1842	**Re-enact.**	5-6 Vic., c.lxxiv
1874	**Ann. Cont. Act**	37-8 Vic., c.95

(**To expire:** 1 Nov. 1874)

The Act of 27 Geo.II was the authorising Act of the Leicester to Hinckley, etc. trust (no. 12). It is included here as it contained a clause rectifying an omission in the toll list of the first Act for this road.

9

Ashby de la Zouch to Burton on Trent and the Cock Inn, Tutbury
(later became the A50)

1753	**Act of 1st Auth.**	26 Geo.II, c.85
1778-9	**Cont. Act**	19 Geo.III, c.85
1801-2	**Cont. Act**	42 Geo.III, c. xliv
1824	**Re-enact.**	5 Geo.IV, c.ci

Fig. 29: The toll house at Ashby on the A50 in 1947.

1867-8	**Ann. Cont. Act**	31-2 Vic., c.99

(Sched. nearly out of debt. 1866 tolls £1258, debt £150, interest 5 per cent)

1870	**Ann. Cont. Act**	33-4 Vic., c.73

(Sched. out of debt)

1872	**Ann. Cont. Act**	35-6 Vic., c.85

(**To expire:** 31 Dec. 1872)

Fig. 30: A milestone on the Leicester to Uppingham road.

10

Leicester to Peterborough, via the north side of Uppingham and Wansford
(later became the A47)

1753-4	**Act of 1st Auth.**	27 Geo.II, c.30
1774	**Cont. Act**	14 Geo.III, c.113
1800-1	**Re-enact.**	41 Geo.III, c.cxviii
1822	**Re-enact.**	3 Geo.IV, c.xlvi
1843	**Re-enact.**	6-7 Vic., c.xcvi
1872	**Ann. Cont. Act**	35-6 Vic., c.85

(Wansford and Peterborough District:
To expire: 1 May 1873;
Leicester District: mod. from 1 Nov. 1872: repairs limited to £400, interest limited to 1 per cent,
To expire: 1 Nov. 1876;
Uppingham District: mod. from 1 Nov. 1872: repairs limited to £150, interest limited to 1 per cent, **To expire:** 1 Nov. 1876.)

By the 1822 Act the Peterborough terminus was defined as at the Market Place. The districts were defined as follows:
1st Division, Leicester to the Leicestershire boundary; 2nd Division (Upper), the Leicestershire boundary to Wansford; Peterborough Division, all the remainder. By the 1843 Act the Leicester terminus was defined as at the south-east end of Curzon Street.

North end of Bridgford Lane, near Trent Bridge, Nottingham, to the Bowling Green, Kettering, via Melton Mowbray, Oakham, Uppingham and Rockingham

(later became the A606 and A6003)

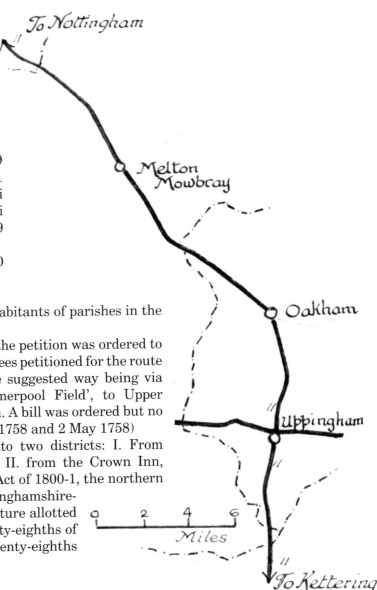

1753-4	**Act of 1st Auth.**	27 Geo.II, c.39
1779-80	**Cont. Act**	20 Geo.III, c.81
1800-1	**Re-enact.**	41 Geo.III, c.cxvii
1823	**Cont. Act**	4 Geo.IV, c.lvi
1868	**Ann. Cont. Act**	31-2 Vic., c.99
(out of debt)		
1873	**Ann. Cont. Act**	36-7 Vic., c.90

(**To expire:** 1 Nov. 1873)

See page 24 for notes on exemptions for the inhabitants of parishes in the Vale of Belvoir, etc. at the Melton Mowbray gate.

Alterations of powers were sought in 1758, but the petition was ordered to lie on the table. A few months later some of the trustees petitioned for the route to be altered in the Nottinghamshire portion, the suggested way being via Plumtree and Stanton Lane 'leading into Widmerpool Field', to Upper Broughton, instead of via Plumtree and Normanton. A bill was ordered but no further action is recorded. (HCJ, 31 Geo.II, 11 Feb.1758 and 2 May 1758)

From the first Act, this road was divided into two districts: I. From Bridgford Lane to the Crown Inn, Oakham, and II. from the Crown Inn, Oakham, to the Bowling Green, Kettering. By the Act of 1800-1, the northern section was further divided at the Nottinghamshire-Leicestershire boundary, and the shares of expenditure allotted as follows: north end of north district, eleven twenty-eighths of two thirds; south end of north district, seventeen twenty-eighths of two thirds, south district, one third.

12

Leicester to Narborough; Leicester to Earl Shilton, Hinckley, Nuneaton, Coventry, Warwick and Halford Bridge; Warwick to Stratford on Avon; Coventry to Martyn's Gutter
(later became the A47 and a section of the A46)

| 1753-4 | **Act of 1st Auth.** | 27 Geo.II, c.42 |

12 A. Hinckley to Nuneaton and Coventry

1755-6	**Amend. (Section)**	29 Geo.II, c.66
1761-2	**Cont. Act**	2 Geo.III, c.69
1805	**Revival** and **Cont. Act**	45 Geo.III, c1
1825	**Re-enact.**	6 Geo.IV, c.x
1878	**Ann. Cont. Act**	41-2 Vic., c.62
(To expire: 1 Nov. 1879)		

12 B. Leicester to Hinckley, via Earl Shilton; Leicester to Narborough.

1768-9	**Amend. (Section)**	8-9 Geo.III, sess. 2 c.91
1799-1800	**Re-enact.**	39-40 Geo.III, c.iii
1821	**Cont. Act**	1-2 Geo.IV, c.ix
1842	**Re-enact.**	5-6 Vic., c.lxx
1874	**Ann. Cont. Act**	37-8 Vic., c.95
(To expire: 1 Nov. 1874)		

Martyn's Gutter marked the boundary between Coventry and Stivichall, on the road to Stoneleigh. It was also on the boundary between the old County of the City of Coventry and the County of Warwick proper.

The Act of 27 Geo. II also contained a clause amending the Leicester to Ashby Act of the previous session. (See No. 8). The trustees of that Act were also the petitioners for this.

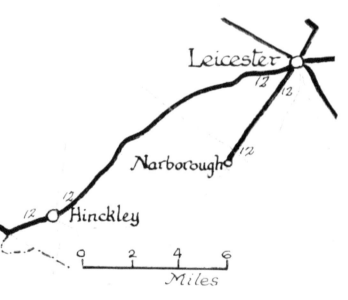

The 1842 Act defined the termini of this road as:

Leicester, Narborough road:
> the Hinckley and Narborough guide post in
> Bromkinsthorpe

Leicester, Hinckley road:
> 100 yards west of Bromkinsthorpe Bridge in
> Braunstone Gate

Narborough:
> the commencement of the village;

Hinckley:
> the 13th milestone from Leicester;

Earl Shilton:
> both ends of the village street, i.e. the streets of the
> village were not under the control of the trust

The other sections of the road, not in Leicestershire, were continued by separate series of Acts, as follows:

Coventry to Warwick; Coventry to Martyn's Gutter:

1775-6	**Cont. Act (Section)**	16 Geo.III, c.81
1795-6	**Cont. Act**	36 Geo.III, c.133
1817	**Re-enact.**	57 Geo.III, c.iv
1841	**Re-enact.**	4-5 Vic., c.xxxiv
1872	**Ann. Cont. Act**	35-6 Vic., c.85

(Mod. from 1 Nov. 1872: repairs limited to £300 p.a., interest limited to 2 per cent. **To expire:** 1 Nov. 1875)

Warwick to Paddle Brook (substituted for Halford Bridge); Warwick to Stratford on Avon.

1779-80	**Re-enact. (Section)**	20 Geo.III, c.71
1806	**Re-enact.**	46 Geo.III, c.xlvii
1826-7	**Re-enact.**	7-8 Geo.IV, c.xxvi
1870	**Ann. Cont. Act**	33-4 Vic., c.73

(Sched. out of debt)

1872	**Ann. Cont. Act**	35-6 Vic., c.85

(**To expire:** 1 Nov. 1872)

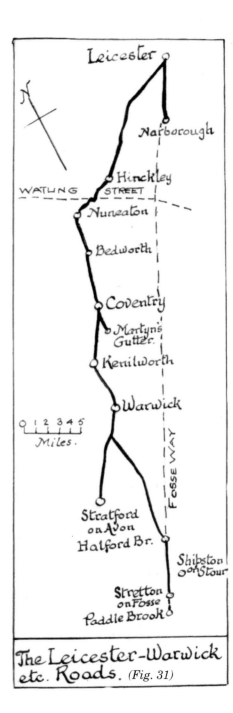

The Leicester-Warwick etc. Roads. *(Fig. 31)*

13

Market Harborough to Coventry, via Lutterworth
(later became the A427 and A4114)

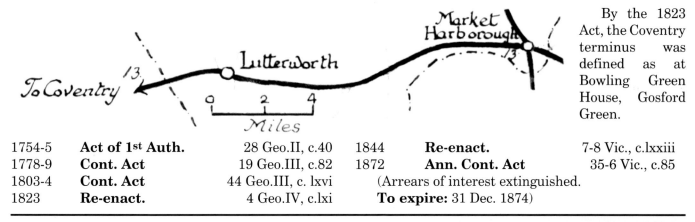

By the 1823 Act, the Coventry terminus was defined as at Bowling Green House, Gosford Green.

1754-5	**Act of 1st Auth.**	28 Geo.II, c.40	1844	**Re-enact.**	7-8 Vic., c.lxxiii
1778-9	**Cont. Act**	19 Geo.III, c.82	1872	**Ann. Cont. Act**	35-6 Vic., c.85
1803-4	**Cont. Act**	44 Geo.III, c. lxvi		(Arrears of interest extinguished.	
1823	**Re-enact.**	4 Geo.IV, c.lxi		**To expire:** 31 Dec. 1874)	

14

Burleigh Bridge, Loughborough, to Ashby de la Zouch via Grace Dieu and Cole Orton; (south end of Grace Dieu Lane to Talbot Lane, via south end of Thringstone)
(later became the A512)

1756-7	**Act of 1st Auth.**	30 Geo.II, c.44

Also including Cole Orton to Rempstone.

1761-2	**Cont. Act**	2 Geo.II, c.82
1798-9	**Cont. Act**	39 Geo.III, c.xlvii
1821	**Cont. Act**	1-2 Geo.IV, c.xxxix
1863	**Re-enact.**	26-7 Vic., c.liii
1866, 10 July	Amalgamated with No.4 A	
1884	**Ann. Cont. Act**	47-8 Vic., c.52

(United roads **Repealed:** 25 Mar. 1885)

The Thringstone branch is mentioned in the petition for the first Act but seems to have been omitted from the Acts themselves, except the last (1863), which refers to it as 'the existing branch'.

The Act of 1798-9 contains the record of an agreement between the trustees of this road and that of the Tamworth and Sawley road (No. 17), by which the latter had to repair the section between Ashby de la Zouch and the entrance to Swarcliffe Lane, i.e. the junction now known as 'Cole Orton turn'. The section, says the Act, 'has never been properly repaired'. It was, however, definitely the responsibility of the Loughborough to Ashby trust, as the Tamworth to Sawley Acts explicitly omit it. (See No. 17). Despite the agreement, the titles of the later Acts of both trusts continue as previously.

The amalgamation of 1866 was effected under the provisions of the Act, 12-13 Vic., c.46, An Act to Facilitate the Union of Turnpike Trusts, 1849.

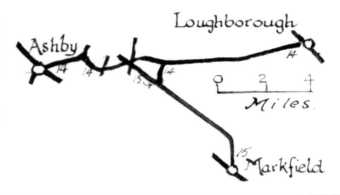

15

Markfield Turnpike, over Charnwood Forest, to the Loughborough to Ashby road, near Snape Gate, via Whitwick, and through Talbot Lane
(later became the B587)

1756-7	**Act of 1st Auth.**	30 Geo.II, c.49	The petitioners for the first Act were the trustees of the Leicester to Ashby road (No. 8)
1782-3	**Revival** and **Cont. Act**	23 Geo.III, c.107	
1805	**Cont. Act**	45 Geo.III, c.lxxix	This road seems to have lapsed as a turnpike. No record appears to exist of the renewal or repeal of the 1826 Act.
1826	**Re-enact.**	7 Geo.IV, c.cxxxiv	

16

Grantham to Trent Bridge, Nottingham, via Bottesford; Chapel Bar, Nottingham, to St. Mary's Bridge, Derby; Lenton to Sawley Ferry
(later became the A52)

1758-9	**Act of 1st Auth.**	32 Geo.II, c.53	1855, 17 Dec. **Prov. Order**.

16A. Grantham to Trent Bridge only.

(Debt £10,535 2s., interest reduced to 3 per cent arrears of interest extinguished to 27 January 1856.)

1766-7	**Cont. Act (Section)**	7 Geo.III, c. 79	1856	**ATTA Act** 19-20 Vic., c.12
1805	**Cont. Act**	45 Geo.III, c.xxxv		(Confirmation of above Prov. Order)
1825	**Re-enact.**	6 Geo.IV, c.xxiv	1876	**Ann. Cont. Act** 39-40 Vic., c.39

(**To expire:** 1 Nov. 1876)

The petition for the 1766-7 Act asked for the inclusion of two branches: Bingham to east end of a lane between Lowdham and Bulcote, via Gunthorpe Ferry, and east end of Radcliffe Field to Stoke Ferry; (HCJ Geo. III, 27 Jan.) No mention of these is made in the Act.

The other sections of the original roads, in Nottinghamshire and Derbyshire, were continued by a separate series of Acts, as follows:

Chapel Bar, Nottingham, to Derby;
Lenton to Sawley Ferry.

1779-80	**Cont. Act (Section)**	20 Geo.III, c.73
1798-9	**Cont. Act**	39 Geo.III, c.xii
1819	**Cont. Act**	59 Geo.III, c.vi
1826-7	**Re-enact.**	7-8 Geo.IV, c.xxvii
1867-8	**Ann. Cont. Act**	31-2 Vic., c.99

(Sched. nearly out of debt. 1866: Western Divn. tolls £570, debt £330, 4 per cent; Eastern Divn. tolls £837, debt £250, 4 per cent).

1870	**Ann. Cont. Act**	33-4 Vic., c.73

(Eastern Divn. **To expire:** 1 Nov. 1870)

1871	**Ann. Cont. Act**	34-5 Vic., c.115

(Western Divn. **To expire:** 1 Nov. 1871)

Sawley Ferry was superseded by the Harrington Bridge. (See page 26).

The Act of 1826-7 included short extensions: in Derby, to the New China Works; in Nottingham, to the east end of Chapel Bar.

The Eastern and Western Divisions of this road met at Risley.

Fig. 32: The Lount toll house, at the crossing of Roads 17 and 18.

17

Tamworth to Ashby de la Zouch; Swarcliffe Lane to Sawley Ferry
(later became the A453)

1759-60	**Act of 1st Auth.**	33 Geo.II, c.41	1878	**Ann. Cont. Act**	41-2 Vic., c.62
1780-1	**Cont. Act**	21 Geo.III, c.89		**(Repealed:** 1 Nov. 1880)	
1802-3	**Cont. Act**	43 Geo.III, c.xxviii		Swarcliffe Lane: see note to No.14	
1823	**Re-enact.**	4 Geo.IV, c.cxxii		Sawley Ferry: see page 26	
1863	**Re-enact.**	26-7 Vic., c.clv			

18

Duck Paddle Street, Hinckley, to Woeful Bridge, Tonge, via Cadeby, Osbaston, Ibstock, Hoo Ash Lane and Breedon Brand; north end of Hoo Ash Lane, via Old Lane, to Lee Gutter; Swannington to Lee Gutter; Lee Gutter to Melbourne Common; Ibstock to Measham; Gelscoe Lane to the turning leading to Belton
(main route later became the A447)

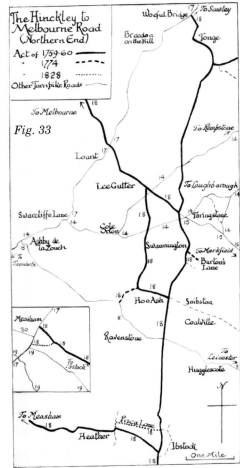

1759-60	**Act of 1st Auth.**	33 Geo.II, c.46

With addition of: Phiney's House, Osbaston, to Cheshire's House, Carlton; Swannington, through Burton's lane, to the Coal Pits; Old Lane to the Leicester to Ashby turnpike road.

1774	**Cont. Act**	14 Geo.III, c.110
1808	**Cont. Act**	44 Geo.III, c.x

With addition of: Pisca Lane (Ibstock and Heather); Green Lane to Measham.

1828	**Re-enact.**	9 Geo.IV, c.v
1859	**Re-enact.**	22-3 Vic., c.1xvii
1878	**Ann. Cont. Act**	41-2 Vic., c.62

(Repealed: 1 Nov. 1878)

The Hinckley to Melbourne Road (Northern End)
Act of 1759-60 ——
" 1774 – – – –
" 1828 ·········
Other Turnpike Roads ———

Fig. 33

Fig. 34

Arrangement of Tolls,

TO BE TAKEN ON THE

HINCKLEY AND MELBOURN

TURNPIKE ROAD.

From HINCKLEY to WOEFUL BRIDGE.

Carriages, Horses, &c. passing first through Hinckley gate pay a full toll—go free through Stapleton gate or bars—pay a half toll at Cadeby Machine gate—a full toll at Osbaston gate—a full toll at Pisca Lane bar or gate—go free through Hoo Ash gate—pay a half toll at Froggatt's Lane or Engine gate—and a full toll at Redwood gate.

Carriages, Horses, &c. passing first through Stapleton gate or bar pay a full toll—go free through Cadeby Machine gate—pay a full toll at Osbaston gate—a full toll at Pisca Lane bar or gate—go free through Hoo Ash gate—pay a half toll at Froggatt's Lane or Engine gate—and a full toll at Redwood gate.

Carriages, Horses, &c. passing first through Cadeby Machine gate pay a full toll—a half toll at Osbaston gate—a full toll at Pisca Lane bar or gate—go free through Hoo Ash gate—pay a half toll at Froggatt's Lane or Engine gate—and a full toll at Redwood gate.

Carriages, Horses, &c. passing first through Osbaston bars or gate, or Belcher's bar, pay a full toll—a full toll at Pisca Lane bar or gate—go free through Hoo Ash gate—pay a half toll at Froggatt's Lane or Engine gate—and a full toll at Redwood gate.

Carriages, Horses, &c. passing first through Pisca Lane gate or bar pay a full toll—go free through Hoo Ash gate—pay a half toll at Old Lane, Froggatt's Lane, or Engine gate—and a full toll at Redwood gate.

Carriages, Horses, &c. passing first through Hoo Ash gate pay a full toll—a half toll at Froggatt's Lane or Engine gate—and a full toll at Redwood gate.

Carriages, Horses, &c. passing first through Froggatt's Lane or Engine gate pay a full toll, and a full toll at Redwood gate.

From WOEFUL BRIDGE to HINCKLEY.

Carriages, Horses, &c. passing first through Redwood gate pay a full toll—a half toll at Newbold gate—a half toll at Froggatt's Lane or Engine gate—a full toll at Hoo Ash gate—go free through Pisca Lane bar—pay a full toll at Pisca Lane gate—a full toll at Belcher's bar or Osbaston gate or bars—a half toll at Cadeby Machine gate—go free through Stapleton bar or gate, and pay a full toll at Hinckley gate.

Carriages, Horses, &c. passing first through Froggatt's Lane or Engine gate pay a full toll—a full toll at Hoo Ash gate—go free through Pisca Lane bar—pay a full toll at Pisca Lane gate—a full toll at Belcher's bar or Osbaston gate or bars—a half toll at Cadeby Machine gate—go free through Stapleton bar or gate, and pay a full toll at Hinckley gate.

Carriages, Horses, &c. passing first through Hoo Ash gate pay a full toll—go free through Pisca Lane bar—pay a full toll at Pisca Lane gate—a full toll at Belcher's bar or Osbaston gate or bars—a half toll at Cadeby Machine gate—go free through Stapleton bar or gate, and pay a full toll at Hinckley gate.

Carriages, Horses, &c. passing first through Pisca Lane bar or gate pay a full toll—a full toll at Belcher's bar or Osbaston gate or bars—a half toll at Cadeby Machine gate—go free through Stapleton bar or gate—and pay a full toll at Hinckley gate.

Carriages, Horses, &c. passing first through Belcher's bar or Osbaston gate pay a full toll—a half toll at Cadeby Machine gate—go free through Stapleton bar or gate—and pay a full toll at Hinckley gate.

Carriages, Horses, &c. passing first through Cadeby Machine gate pay a full toll—go free through Stapleton bar or gate—and pay a half toll at Hinckley gate.

Carriages, Horses, &c. passing first through Stapleton bar or gate pay a full toll, and go free through Hinckley gate.

From HINCKLEY to MELBOURN COMMON.

Carriages, Horses, &c. passing first through Hoo Ash gate pay a full toll—a half toll at Cartbrook bar—go free through Old Lane and Newbold gate—and pay a full toll at Staunton bar or gate.

Carriages, Horses, &c. passing first through Old Lane gate pay a full toll—a half toll at Cartbrook bar—go free through Newbold and Hoo Ash gates—and pay a full toll at Staunton bar or gate.

Carriages, Horses, &c. passing first through Cartbrook bar pay a full toll—go free through Newbold gate—and pay a full toll at Staunton bar or gate.

Carriages, Horses, &c. passing first through Newbold Gate pay a full toll, and a half toll at Staunton bar or gate.

Carriages, Horses, &c. passing first through Engine gate pay a full toll—go free through Newbold gate—and pay a full toll at Staunton bar or gate.

From MELBOURN COMMON to HINCKLEY.

Carriages, Horses, &c. passing first through Staunton gate or bar pay a full toll—go free through Newbold gate—pay a full toll at Engine gate or Cartbrook bar—and a half toll at Old Lane or Hoo Ash gate.

Carriages, Horses, &c. passing first through Newbold gate pay a full toll—go free through Cartbrook bar or Engine gate—pay a full toll at Old Lane or Hoo Ash gate.

Carriages, Horses, &c. passing first through Cartbrook bar pay a full toll, and a half toll at Old Lane or Hoo Ash gate.

From HINCKLEY to MEASHAM.

Carriages, Horses, &c. passing first through Osbaston bars or gate pay a full toll—go free through Belcher's bar—pay a half toll at Heather Mill bar—and a full toll at Swepstone bar or gate.

Carriages, Horses, &c. passing first through Belcher's bar, pay a full toll—go free through Heather Mill bar—and pay a full toll at Swepstone bar or gate.

Carriages, Horses, &c. passing first through Heather Mill bar, pay a full toll—and a half toll at Swepstone bar or gate.

From MEASHAM to HINCKLEY.

Carriages, Horses, &c. passing first through Swepstone Gate or bar pay a full toll—a half toll at Heather Mill bar—go free through Belcher's bar—and pay a full toll at Osbaston Gate or bars.

Carriages, horses, &c. passing first through Heather Mill bar pay a full toll—go free through Belcher's bar, and pay a full toll at Osbaston Gate or bars.

Carriages, horses, &c. passing first through Belcher's bar, pay a full toll—and go free through Osbaston Gate or bars.

	s.	d.
For every horse, mule, ass, or other beast of draught, drawing any coach, chaise, marine, barouche, sociable, landau, berlin, cabriolet, phaeton, curricle, gig, chair, whiskey, calash, caravan, hearse, break, sledge, litter, taxed cart, or other such like carriage the sum of	0	4½
For every horse, mule, ass, or other beast of draught, drawing a waggon, wain, cart, or other such carriage, having the fellies of the wheels thereof of the breadth of six inches, the sum of	0	3
For every horse, mule, ass, or other beast of draught, drawing a waggon, wain, cart, or other such carriage, having the fellies of the wheels thereof of the breadth of four inches and a half, and less than six inches, the sum of	0	4
For every horse, mule, ass, or other beast of draught, drawing a waggon, wain, cart, or other such carriage, having the fellies of the wheels thereof of less breadth than four inches and a half, the sum of	0	6
For every ox, cow, or other head of neat cattle, not drawing; the sum of	0	1½
For every calf, hog, sheep, or lamb, the sum of	0	½
For every horse, mule, or ass, or other beast laden or unladen, and not drawing, the sum of	0	1½

T. SHORT, Printer and bookseller, HINCKLEY.

Duck Paddle Street, Hinckley, is now known as Regent Street, and has also been called Coventry Street. (Ex. inf. J.S. Featherstone, Esq., Surveyor to Hinckley UDC)

Pisca Lane is the more northerly of the two roads connecting Ibstock with Heather. (Ex. inf. Revd W.R. Newberry, Ibstock).

Green Lane was, apparently, the Measham end of what is now the main road. The older, pre-1828, entrance to Measham from Ibstock seems to have been half a mile nearer Ashby and is now a footpath. (See map on page 54).

Burton's Lane runs north-westwards from the main road, Swannington, about three-quarters of a mile north of the railway station. (Ex. inf. Reginald H. Smith, Esq., Surveyor to the Coalville UDC and Edgar Hawthorn, Esq., of Coalville).

Summaries of the early petitions and of the proceedings in Parliament leading to the passing of the first Act for this road are contained in the box on pages 12-13. At the other end of its life, page 28 shows a notice of sale of the materials of the toll houses, following its expiration in 1880. Page 56 shows an undated printed notice for the 'Arrangement of tolls'.

19

The bridge, Burton on Trent, to Market Bosworth; Measham to Fieldon Bridge; Tamworth to Market Bosworth; Polesworth to Pinwall Lane; Market Bosworth to Hinckley, via Sutton Cheney and Dadlington; Belchiers to Hoop Hall, Market Bosworth

1759-60	**Act of 1st Auth.**	33 Geo.II, c.47
	With addition of Crickett's Inn to Twycross, via Appleby	
1780-1	**Cont. Act**	21 Geo.III, c.92
1809	**Cont. Act**	49 Geo.III, c.vii

19A. Burton Bridge to Market Bosworth only.

1830-1	**Re-enact. (Section)**	1 Wm.IV, c.x
1867-8	**Ann. Cont. Act**	31-2 Vic., c.99
	(Sched. nearly out of debt. 1866 tolls: £1250, debt £50, interest 5 per cent)	

1870	**Ann. Cont. Act**	33-4 Vic., c.73
(Sched. out of debt)		
1872	**Ann. Cont. Act**	35-6 Vic., c.85

(**To expire:** 1 November 1872)

19B. Measham to Fieldon Bridge; Tamworth to Pinwall Lane, via Polesworth; Crickett's Inn to Twycross via Appleby.

1830-1	**Re-enact. (Section)**	1 Wm.IV, c.xii
1863 17 Feb.	**Prov. Order.**	

Trust to be united with the Watling Street trust (No.22 A) Debt £1, 809, interest reduced to 4 per cent from 1 Jan 1863.

1863	**ATTA Act**	26-7 Vic., c.98
(Confirmation of above Prov. Order)		
1872	**Ann. Cont. Act**	35-6 Vic., c.85

(**To expire:** 31 Dec. 1872)

The original petition also included the road from Polesworth, via Lovatt's Bridge, Sutton Cheney and Peckleton, to the 'most convenient part' of the road between Earl Shilton and Leicester. (HCJ 33 Geo. II, 18 Dec. 1759). It is doubtful if the parts of the road included in the earlier Acts but omitted from those of 1830-1 were ever brought under effective control of the trust.

Enquiries of old residents of the district (through the good offices of Alderman Frank Bouskell, of Market Bosworth), have failed to establish the position of Hoop Hall. The most convenient place for a road from Belchiers (marked on modern maps as Belcher's Bar) to join the roads of this trust seems to be at Carlton, which was in Bosworth parish. If this was the site of Hoop Hall, the road must have been that shown on recent maps as a green lane running south along the boundary between Odstone and Nailstone, and continued as a minor road to Carlton Gate.

This turnpike is cited in objections to road 18 – the Hinckley to Woeful Bridge bill of 1760 (see pages 12-13).

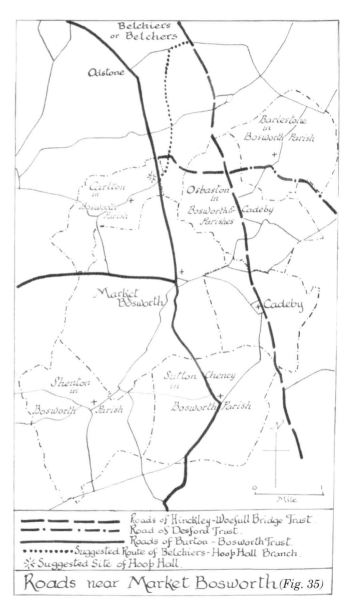

Roads near Market Bosworth (Fig. 35)

20

Castle Street, Hinckley, to Town's End, Lutterworth; Town's End, Walcot, to the 80th milestone, Welford Field
(later the B578 and a short section of the A5)

1761-2	**Act of 1st Auth.**	2 Geo.III, c.54
1783-4	**Cont. Act**	24 Geo.III, Sess. 1 c.28
1805	**Cont. Act**	45 Geo.III, c.xxxvi
	Walcot to Welford Field branch omitted.	
1823	**Re-enact.**	4 Geo.IV, c.1x
1876	**Ann. Cont. Act**	39-40 Vic., c.39
	(To expire: 1 Nov. 1876))	

The early history of this road as a turnpike is bound up with that of the Watling Street road (No. 22) and commences nearly thirty years before the passing of the authorising Act. (See notes to No. 22).

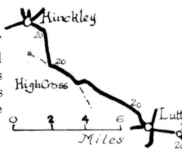

The section of the road between Lutterworth and Walcot was under trust controlling the road from Market Harborough to Coventry (No. 13)

It is doubtful if the Walcot to Welford Field section of this road were ever effectively controlled by the trust, and its omission from the Act of 1823 was evidently a recognition of already existing conditions. The neglect of this section seems strange in view of the fact that it is about two miles shorter than the route actually used at the time and later between the same two points. It was probably due to it having steeper gradients, though the possibility must not be ruled out that it was due to personal influence of the Braye family. The most used route at the end of the eighteenth century seems to have been that in use today, i.e. from Walcot, through North Kilworth to the Canal Wharf, thence past Cote Hill Farm to the Welford to Leicester road (ACCA in fig. 35) A slightly longer route than the turnpike branch (AA) was that now represented by field tracks direct from Welford to North Kilworth (BB) This seems to have been in use as a through road at one time and appears on Laird's map of 1808 as the main road. The present route (CC) was used by the London to Holyhead mails before Telford's improvements caused the transfer to the Coventry and Birmingham road, after which the old Holyhead road was used by the mails between London and Woodside Ferry, Birkenhead.

Roads between Welford and Lutterworth. (Fig. 36)

21

St. James Deeping Stone Bridge to Peter's Gate, Stamford, and the south end of Morcott

1761-2	Act of 1st Auth.	2 Geo.III, c.73
1786	Cont. Act	26 Geo.III, c.159
1806	Cont. Act	46 Geo.III, c.xcix
1829	Re-enact.	10 Geo.IV, c.lxxxviii
1870	Ann. Cont. Act	33-4 Vic., c.73
(Sched. out of debt)		
1872	Ann. Cont. Act	35-6 Vic., c.85
(**To expire:**1 Nov. 1872))		

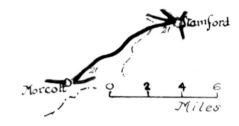

22

'The London to Holyhead Road'
Watling Street, from the Three Pots Inn, Burbage, to Fazeley Bridge (except for the short stretch already turnpiked as part of the Hinckley to Nuneaton road, No. 12); Fieldon Bridge to Bow Bridge, Over Whitacre, via Atherstone; Whitacre Furnace to Nuneaton Common; Mancetter Lane End to Nuneaton Common; Nuneaton Common to Abbey End, Nuneaton; Church Street, Nuneaton, to Wolvey Heath; Coventry to Whitacre

(includes what later became the A5)

1761-2	Act of 1st Auth.	2 Geo.III, c.80
1780-1	Cont. Act	21 Geo.III, c.85
With extension to Blyth Bridge, Whitacre.		
1810	Cont. Act	50 Geo.III, c.cxxxv

22A. As above, except Coventry to Whitacre, and with extensions: Three Pots Inn to the Hinckley to Lutterworth road (No. 20); Wolvey Heath to the Five Lane Ends, Wolvey Heath.

1830-1	Re-enact. (Section)	1 Wm.IV, c.xiv
1863, 17 Feb.	Prov. Order. Trust united with No. 19 B Debt £1,809, interest reduced to 4 per cent from 1 Jan. 1863.	
1863	ATTA Act	26-7 Vic., c.98
(Confirmation of above Prov. Order)		
1868-9	Ann. Cont. Act	32-3 Vic., c.90
(Ansley and Whitacre section: **To expire:** 1 Nov. 1875).		

1872   **Ann. Cont. Act**   35-6 Vic., c.85
    (Mancetter and Wolvey section: mod. from 1 Nov.
    1872: no expenditure on repairs, interest reduced
    to 2 per cent, **To expire:** 1 Nov. 1875.
    Remaining sections, including the Leicestershire
    portions: **To expire:** 31 Dec. 1872.)

The Coventry to Whitacre section, omitted from the
1830-1 Act, was continued as a separate trust, but with
no mileage in Leicestershire, under the following Act:

1830-1   **Re-enact. (Section)**   1 Wm.IV, c.xli
1872   **Ann. Cont. Act**   35-6 Vic., c.85
    (**To expire:** 1 Nov. 1875))

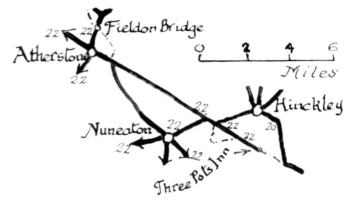

The history of the turnpiking of this group of roads
begins nearly thirty years before the passing of the first
Act. On 20 Feb. 1734, a petition was presented to
Parliament asking for the turnpiking of Watling Street
from Weedon to Fazeley Bridge, with a short branch
from Housewife's Bridge to Nuneaton. Four days later
another petition asked for an Act to cover the road
from Watling Street at High Cross to Lutterworth and
Welford Field. On the same day, in another petition,
these schemes were combined, together with other
roads not previously included. By this proposal,
Nuneaton would be on the direct route, which was to
start at Thorny Lane, near Welford, and reach Fazeley
Bridge by way of Lutterworth, Wolvey, Attleborough,
Nuneaton, Mancetter and Atherstone. These petitions
were referred to a committee and no more is heard of
them. (HCJ, 8 Geo.II, 1734, relevant dates).

The scheme was revived in 1760. On 21 Jan., a
petition was presented asking for the turnpiking of
Watling Street from Fazeley Bridge to Lutterworth
Hand, except for the short piece forming part of the
Hinckley to Nuneaton road, which had been turnpiked
in 1753-4 (No. 12); the roads from the White Lion,
Shustoke, via Atherstone, to Fieldon Bridge; Arbour

Houses, Mancetter, to Nuneaton Common; Over
Whitacre to Nuneaton; and Nuneaton to the Coventry
to Lutterworth road, via Wolvey Heath and Cloudesley
Bush. On 25 Jan., another petition asked for the
inclusion of the road from the Three Pots Inn to Duck
Paddle Street, Hinckley.

Objecting petitions came in during the latter half of
February – from Coventry and Coleshill on 13th,
Meriden in 14th, Daventry on 22nd, and Birmingham
on 27th. Meanwhile, Nuneaton had petitioned in
favour on 22nd. On 21st the trustees of the Dunchurch
to Meriden road had objected. The basis of the contrary
petitions was, of course, the expected loss of trade by
the towns on the existing turnpikes and the loss of
traffic by the trustees operating them and by those
who had lent money to the trusts. The road from Old
Stratford, via Daventry, to Dunchurch had been
turnpiked as long previously as 1706-7 (by 5 Ann.,
c.77), and that from Dunchurch to Meriden in two
stages, to Stonebridge in 1723-4 (by 10 Geo.I, c.15) and
to Meriden in 1753 (by 26 Geo.II, c.73). The combined
opposition was successful and the bill was dropped in
committee. (HCJ, 33 Geo.II, relevant dates).

Two sessions later, further attempts were
successful. On 3 Dec. 1761, a petition was presented to
cover the roads from the Three Pots Inn To Fazeley

Bridge, except for the short stretch previously mentioned; from the Cross Lanes, near Whitacre Furnace, and from Mancetter, to Nuneaton Common and thence to Abbey End, Nuneaton. The inclusion of the road from Coventry to Over Whitacre; Bentley Lane; and the road over Baddesley Common to Watling Street and thence to Polesworth were asked for on 13 Feb. The road from Church Street, Nuneaton, to Wolvey Heath was the subject of a further petition on 19 Feb.

On 8 March 1762 the report stage was reached. Among the witnesses examined by the committee was John Hewitt, appearing on behalf of the petition of 13 Feb. He said the Coventry to Whitacre road was ruinous, and turnpiking it would be a great advantage to Coventry, as coal could be brought that way from pits where it was sold at 4*d.* per cwt. This would prevent a monopoly by the Bedworth Colliery, the nearest to the city, where coals were 'near 7*d.* per hundred at the pit'. Lime could be brought back, he said, as 'back carriage' to manure the land.

Comparison with the statement of routes at the head of this section will show that all the roads petitioned for 3 Dec., 13 Feb., and 19 Feb. were included in the Act, except for the Polesworth branch. The other part of the old 1734 schemes, from High

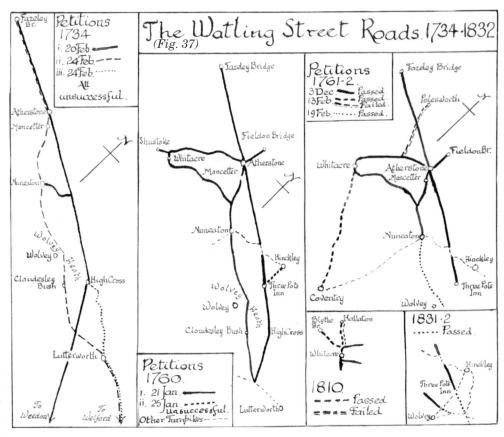

Cross to Lutterworth and Welford Field was revived at the same session and successfully passed through Parliament as a separate concern (See No. 20) (HCJ, 2 Geo.III, relevant dates).

The extension to Blyth Bridge, included in the 1810 renewal, was the result of a petition which also included another extension from Cross Heath to Hallaton, Kingsbury. (HCJ, 50 Geo.III, 7 Feb.1810).

Two further extensions were made at the time of the division of the trust in 1830-1, as can be seen from the maps and statement of routes given above .

23

Melton Mowbray to the guide post in St. Margaret's Fields, Leicester; Round Hill, Barkby, to Barkby village; Leicester to Lutterworth

(includes what later became the A601)

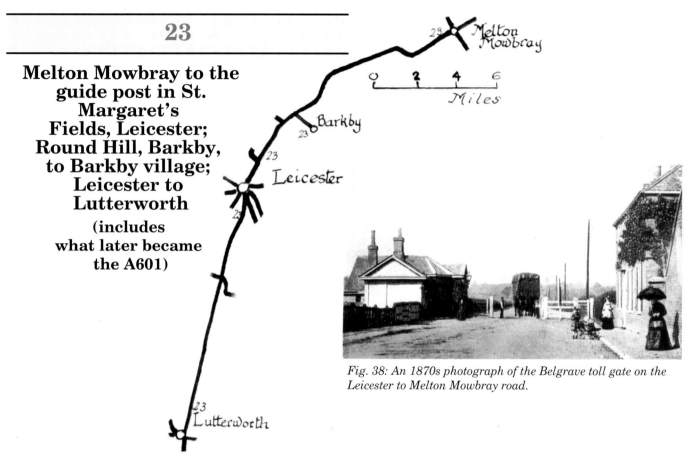

Fig. 38: An 1870s photograph of the Belgrave toll gate on the Leicester to Melton Mowbray road.

| 1763-4 | **Act of 1st Auth.** | 4 Geo.III, c.84 |
| 1785 | **Cont. Act** | 25 Geo.III, c.113 |

23A. Melton Mowbray to Leicester; Round Hill, Barkby, to Barkby village.

1805	**Re-enact. (Section)**	45 Geo.III, c.xlix
1825	**Re-enact.**	6 Geo.IV, c.lxxxi
1867-8	**Ann. Cont. Act**	31-2 Vic., c.99
(Sched. out of debt)		
1870	**Ann. Cont. Act**	33-4 Vic., c.73
(Sched. out of debt)		

| 1872 | **Ann. Cont. Act** | 35-6 Vic., c.85 |
| (**To expire:** 1 Nov 1872) | | |

23B. Leicester to Lutterworth.

1805	**Re-enact. (Section)**	45 Geo.III, c.lxxviii
1825	**Re-enact.**	6 Geo.IV, c.lxxx
1870	**Ann. Cont. Act**	33-4 Vic., c.73
(Sched. nearly out of debt. 1869 tolls £697, debt £198, interest 5 per cent).		
1872	**Ann. Cont. Act**	35-6 Vic., c.85
(**To expire:** 1 Nov 1872)		

24

Welford Bridge to Millstone Lane, Leicester
(later became the A50)

1765	**Act of 1st Auth.**	5 Geo.III, c.78
1786	**Cont. Act**	26 Geo.III, c.148
1805	**Re-enact.**	45 Geo.III, c.lxxviii
1825	**Re-enact.**	6 Geo.IV, c.lxxxii
1878	**Ann. Cont. Act**	41-2 Vic., c.62

(To expire: 1 Nov. 1878)

26

(i) Scot Gate, Stamford, to Oakham; Oakham to Booth's Gate, Burley, adjoining the open fields of Cottesmore
1772-3 **Act of 1st Auth.**   13 Geo.III, c.108

(ii). Stamford to the Great North Road, at the Cross Guns, Greetham, via Oakham
(later became the A606 and B688)

25

Banbury to the south end of Mill Field, Lutterworth, via Daventry and Cotesbach
(later became the A426)

1765	**Act of 1st Auth.**	5 Geo.III, c.105
1785	**Cont. Act**	25 Geo.III, c.128
1807	**Cont. Act**	47 Geo.III, sess.2 c.xci
1828	**Re-enact.**	9 Geo.IV, c.lxxxvi

With addition of Badby Bridge to the Old Stratford to Dunchurch road at or near Dodford Lane.

| 1840 | **Re-enact.** | 3-4 Vic., c.xxxviii |
| 1867-8 | **Ann. Cont. Act** | 31-2 Vic., c.99 |

(Sched. out of debt)

| 1870 | **Ann. Cont. Act** | 33-4 Vic., c.73 |

(Repealed: 31 May 1871)

1794-5	**Act of 1st Auth.**	35 Geo.III, c.152
1817	**Cont. Act**	57 Geo.III, c.xlvi
1867-8	**Ann. Cont. Act**	31-2 Vic., c.99

(Sched. out of debt)

| 1871 | **Ann. Cont. Act** | 34-5 Vic., c.115 |

(To expire: 1 Nov. 1871)

The first of these Acts seems to have expired without renewal, and that of 1794-5 substituted. In the petition for the last mentioned there is no reference to any previous Act. Its terms are those of an ordinary primary petition, not those for renewal.

27

Sage Cross, Melton Mowbray, to Grantham
(later became the A607)

1779-80	**Act of 1st Auth.**	20 Geo.III, c.95
1800-1	**Cont. Act**	41 Geo.III, c.lxxxvii
1823	**Re-enact.**	4 Geo.IV, c.1
1873	**Ann. Cont. Act**	36-7 Vic., c.90

(Mod. from 1 Nov. 1873: no expenditure on repairs, no interest payable, salaries limited to £20. **To expire:** 1 Nov. 1875 or earlier if bonded debt paid off)

The 1823 Act defined the Grantham terminus as at the north-east side of Sandpit Lane, between the townships of Grantham and Spittlegate.

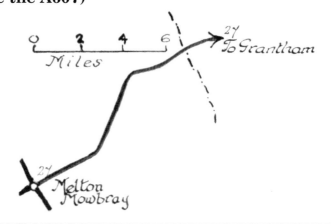

28

Foston Lane on the Leicester to Welford road, via Desford, to Osbaston on the Hinckley to Melbourne road
(later became the B582)

1787-8	**Act of 1st Auth.**	28 Geo.III, c.100
1790	**Cont. Act**	30 Geo.III, c.92
1830-1	**Re-enact.**	1 Wm.IV, c.xxxviii
1863	**Re-enact.**	26-7 Vic., c.xxxiv
1874	**Ann. Cont. Act**	37-8 Vic., c.95

(**To expire:** 1 Nov. 1874)

By the second Act, Hunt's Lane, Desford, and Wood Lane, Newbold Verdon, were added, but they were not mentioned in that of 1863. Hunt's Lane seems to be now the main road through Desford. I have been unable to identify Wood Lane. It is possible that there was a doubt as to the exact route to be taken through the two parishes, and that the second Act was passed to make good the deficiency.

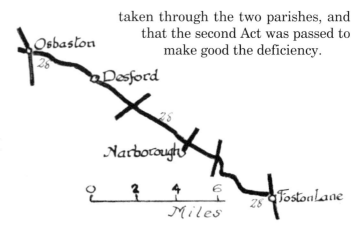

29

Foot of St. Mary's Bridge, Little Bowden, to the west side of the tollbar at north end of Rockingham
(later became the A427)

1792-3	**Act of 1st Auth.**	33 Geo.III, c.143
1812-3	**Cont. Act**	53 Geo.III, c.iv
1835	**Re-enact.**	5-6 Wm.IV, c.xix

1854, 7 Jan., **Prov. Order.**
(Debt £2,728, interest reduced to 3 per cent, arrears extinguished to 1 Jan. 1853)

1854	**ATTA Act**	17-8 Vic., c.51

(Confirmation of above Prov. Order)

1875	**Ann. Cont. Act**	38-9 Vic., c.cxciv

(**Repealed:** 1 Mar. 1876)

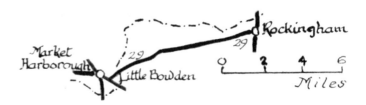

This record was wholly in Northamptonshire until the inclusion of Little Bowden in Leicestershire.

30

The Moira and Gresley Roads

(a) Scaddow Gate, Ticknall, to Wooden Box via Hartshorn.

(b) Wooden Box, over Ashby Woulds, to Clark's Brambury Barn.

(c) Carter's Slade Pond, on (b), to Overseal Upper Lane.

(d) From (b) on Ashby Woulds to Lower or Short Heath Overseal Lane.

(e) Wooden Box over Ashby Woulds, Swadlincote and Gresley Commons, along the Bumby Road to Cadeby Hill.

1794	**Act of 1st Auth.**	34 Geo.III, c.120

Also including

(f) Continuation of (d) to the Burton to Bosworth road, Overseal.

(g) From (b), near where the Short Heath road runs into it, to the Burton to Ashby road, near Ashby de la Zouch.

(h) From (a) at Bull's Head, to the Burton to Ashby road at Smisby Lane Gate.

1815	**Cont. Act**	55 Geo.III, c.lxiii.

Also including:

(i) Extension of (b) to Measham.

(j) Gresley Common on (e), through Gresley, to Linton.

(k) From (j) in Town Street, Linton, to the highway leading from Caldwell to Rosliston, and thence to the junction of roads from Caldwell and Coton to Rosliston.

1834   **Re-enact.**   4-5 Wm.IV, c.lx

With omission of (h) and addition of:
(l) Near Wooden Box near Box Extra on (b), to Linton Heath, near Swain's Park.
(m) From (b) to (l) and thence to the Ashby and Church Gresley boundary.

1864   **Re-enact.**   27-8 Vic., c.lxx
1884-5   **Ann. Cont. Act**   48-9 Vic., c.37
    (Repealed: 1 Nov. 1885)

The descriptions given above have been simplified from the original wording of the Acts, and a few errors may have crept in, owing to the great differences between conditions in the district now and when the earlier Acts were passed. Indeed there have been many alterations in quite recent years (See map right).

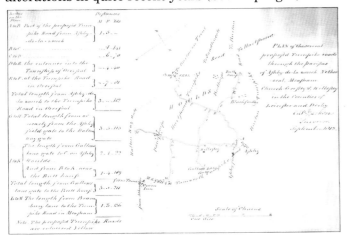

Fig. 39: Proposed turnpikes west of Ashby, surveyed by E.S. Jackson in 1812.

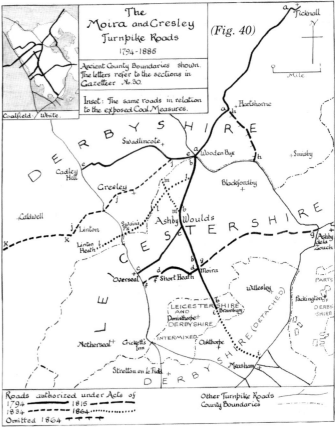

There have been extensive changes in the boundaries of the parishes and townships of the area, and the exchanges of territory between Leicestershire and Derbyshire, all designed to rationalise a complex pattern in which tiny detached parts of parishes were isolated in parts of others, and in which one township had lands in four parishes and two counties. The enclosure of Ashby Woulds and the industrialisation of much of the neighbourhood have added to the difficulties of comparing the 'lay-out' of former days with the modern map (See box on page 69-70 and figure 42).

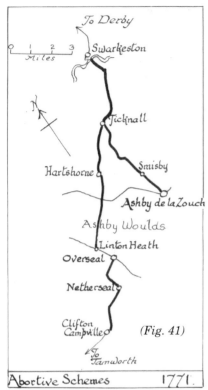

Abortive Schemes   1771.

(Fig. 41)

Wooden Box was a toll house on the Ashby to Burton road. The village which grew up near by took the same name but this has been 'genteelized' into Woodville.

A previous attempt to place roads in this area under trust control took place in 1771. On 31 January in that year a petition was presented to the House of Commons for an Act to cover the following roads: south-east end of Swarkeston Bridge, via Ticknall, Hartshorn, Ashby Woulds, etc., to the road between Burton and Overseal at the top of Linton Heath; from near the Pinfold, Overseal, down Gunby, through Netherseal, to the road at the south-east end of Clifton, leading thence to Clifton Heath; from Ticknall, over the Priston Hills to the north end of Ashby de la Zouch. This was referred to a committee but no further entry occurs (HCJ, relevant date)
(See figure 41 above).

31

Rugby to North Kilworth
(later became the A427)

1801   **Act of 1st Auth.**   41 Geo.III, c.lxxxiii
1825   **Re-enact.**   4 Geo.IV, c.lxiii R
1856, 15 May, **Prov. Order.**
    Debt £1,119 3s 4d, interest reduced to 3 per cent per cent, arrears extinguished to 31 Dec. 1855
1857   **ATTA Act**   20-1 Vic., c.9
    (Confirmation of above Prov. Order)
1873   **Ann. Cont. Act**   36-7 Vic., c.90
(Mod. from 1 Nov. 1873: trust to be amalgamated with the Rugby to Lutterworth and Rugby to Hinckley trusts; repairs for united trusts not to be less than £550 or more than £650; salaries and legal charges not to exceed £90; interest limited to 2 per cent; arrears extinguished; **To expire:** 1 Nov. 1878.)

The Rugby to Hinckley road appears as No.32 in this list. The Rugby to Lutterworth road, despite its name, was not actually a Leicestershire road, its northern terminus being at Lutterworth Hand on Watling Street. The section between the Hand and Lutterworth town was a part of a road from Banbury (No.25). The following is a summary of its Acts:

Lutterworth Hand (Gibbet Hill), via Churchover, and Rugby, to the Cock (or Cock Robin) Inn, Bilton, on the Dunchurch to Northampton road.

1785   **Act of 1st Auth.**   25 Geo.III, c.115
1806   **Cont. Act**   46 Geo. III, c.xxviii
1828   **Re-enact.**   9 Geo.IV, c. lxxxviii
With extension from the Cock Inn to Dunchurch (transferred from the Dunchurch to Northampton trust).
1837-8   **Re-enact.**   1-2 Vic., c.lxxv
1873   **Ann. Cont. Act**   36-7 Vic., c.90
(Mod. and date of expiry as given above, No. 31).

32

The Bridge, Rugby, to Hinckley
(later became the A447 out of Hinckley and B4112)

1812	**Act of 1st Auth.**	52 Geo.III, c.lxxxii
1833	**Re-enact.**	3-4 Wm.IV, c.lxxxvii
1873	**Ann. Cont. Act**	36-7 Vic., c.90

(Mod. and date of expiry as given above, No. 31)
See also figure 5 on page 14

33

'The Fosse Way'
The side gate, Burbage, to the Leicester turnpike road in Narborough
(later became the B4455 and A46)

1813-4	**Act of 1st Auth.**	54 Geo.III, c.xxiv
1835	**Re-enact.**	5-6 Wm.IV, c.lxxix
1867-8	**Ann. Cont. Act**	31-2 Vic., c.99

(Sched. out of debt)

1874	**Ann. Cont. Act**	37-8 Vic., c.95

(**To expire:** 1 Nov. 1874)

34

Coventry to the Hinckley to Narborough road, near Stoney Stanton
(later became the A46)

1830-1	**Act of 1st Auth.**	1Wm.IV, c.xl
1863, 19 Jan.	**Prov. Order.**	

(Non-preferential debt £1750, interest reduced to one penny per £100 from 31 Dec. 1862, arrears extinguished)

1863	**ATTA Act**	26-7 Vic., c.98

(Confirmation of above Prov. Order)

1872	**Ann. Cont. Act**	35-6 Vic., c.85

(Mod. from 1 Nov. 1872: repairs limited to £200, salaries limited to £30 interest limited to 1 per cent. **To expire**: 1 Nov. 1874)

Boundary Changes

Some places mentioned in this publication may be found described in original documents as being in Derbyshire though they are now included in Leicestershire. The following is an attempt at a brief summary of the more important changes which took place in the boundaries of the latter county in the nineteenth century in attempts to rationalize what had been an extremely complicated area.

The parishes chiefly affected were Church Gresley, Measham, Seal, Stretton en le Field, Appleby, Packington and Ravenstone. Before these changes took place there was a large detached part of Derbyshire, comprising the parishes of Measham, Stretton en le Field, Chilcote and a part of Appleby, and several smaller detached pieces around and in Packington, Ravenstone and Appleby. There was also the area of intermixed lands around Donisthorpe, where parts of the parishes of Church Gresley, Seal, Stretton and Measham were in higgledy-piggledy juxtaposition. Separating this detached area from the main part of Derbyshire was the part of Leicestershire which included the parish of Seal and that of part of Ashby de la Zouch forming Ashby Woulds. The whole of Church Gresley parish was in Derbyshire, comprising the townships of Church and Castle Gresley, Swadlincote, Linton and Drakelow, and some of the strips of Derbyshire land in the joint township of Oakthorpe and Donisthorpe. Measham too was in Derbyshire, its parish consisting of the township of Measham in the detached part of its county, and also some of the strips of Oakthorpe and Donisthorpe. Seal parish, comprising the townships of Overseal and Netherseal, was in Leicestershire, and also included some of the Oakthorpe and Donisthorpe strips. Stretton en le Field was in a similar position to Measham.

The combined township of Oakthorpe and Donisthorpe was then an intermixture of parts of four parishes in two counties. As to the origin of this state of things, I can only suggest the following explanation. The inhabitants of Oakthorpe and Donisthorpe, I should imagine, were tenants of four different lords and had their lands intermixed in the same area of open field, common pasture and common meadow. The four lords built churches in the townships where their main land holdings were, that is in Gresley, Measham, Stretton and Seal, and endowed them with the tithes payable to the church by their tenantry including those arising from crops grown in the intermixed open fields. As a man's parish was that to whose incumbent he paid his tithes, it would follow that the four parishes would be represented in the fields of Oakthorpe and Donisthorpe in the same manner as that in which the ownership or tenancy of strips was intermingled in any open field township. A further complication, I submit, was that the lord of Seal owed his civil duty to the Crown through the Sheriff of Leicestershire while the lords of the other three places owed theirs through the Sheriff of Derbyshire. Thus, not only were the parishes mingled, but the counties as well.

The first steps in rationalization seem to have been the consolidation of Oakthorpe and Donisthorpe by forming them into an ecclesiastical parish in 1838. In 1884 the Derbyshire fragments in Packington were amalgamated with the Leicestershire portion; another fragment of Packington, already in Leicestershire, but detached from the main part of the parish, was amalgamated with Ravenstone, the Derbyshire portions of which were also added to Leicestershire. In 1897, the large detached part of Derbyshire was exchanged for the intervening part of Leicestershire.

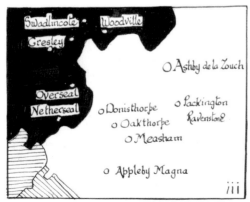

Measham, Chilcote, Stretton en le Field and the whole of Oakthorpe and Donisthorpe were transferred to Leicestershire, as also was the Derbyshire portion of Appleby. Derbyshire acquired the parish of Seal. Meanwhile, a completely new village had sprung up around the Wooden Box tollhouse on the Burton and Ashby road, which to complicate matters was here the county boundary separating the Leicestershire parish of Ashby from the Derbyshire parish of Hartshorne. So, the same Order which exchanged the parts of the two counties was also made to create a new parish from the two sides of the road. It was placed wholly in Derbyshire and received the genteelized title of Woodville.

In another part of the county boundary a change was made under the 1888 Local Government Act by which Little Bowden was transferred from Northamptonshire to Leicestershire. It was later included in the Urban District of Market Harborough.

See maps in figure 42 (left) and figure 25 on page 40.

Fig. 42: Boundary changes on the Leicestershire-Derbyshire border,
 i) the situation pre-1838;
 ii) after the rationalisation of 1884;
 iii) the boundary as it has looked since 1897.

Acknowledgements:

Leicestershire County Council for instigating and grant aiding this publication; Alan Thornton and Leicester City Museums Service for the cover picture; the estate of Arthur Cossons for the photographs on page 2 and figure 29; The Record Office for Leicestershire, Leicester and Rutland for figures 2, 3, 7, 10, 11, 14, 28, 32 (ref. DE 3736), figure 4 (ref. T/Ma/10/4), figure 6 (ref. QS 71/12), figure 15 (ref. T/X/10/10), figure 16 (ref. DE 189/1) and figure 39 (ref. QS 71/5); Peter Stoddart for figures 13 and 30; Snibston Discovery Park for figure 8. All other figures were drawn by Arthur Cossons.

Notes

1 2-3 Ph.&M., c.8 (1555)

2 5 Eliz., c.13 (1562-3)

3 Ordinance of 31 Mar.1654

4 22 Car.II., c.12 (1670)

5 *Calendar of Patent Rolls*, 9 Edw.II (12 Feb 1316)

6 Ibid, 10 Edw.II (13 July 1316)

7 Ibid. 12 Edw.II (24 May 1318)

8 Ibid. 12 Edw.II (25 Aug 1318)

9 Ibid. 14 Edw.II (8 Feb 1321)

10 F.G.Emmison, Turnpike Roads and Tollgates of Bedfordshire, in Bedfordshire Historical Society, *Survey of Ancient Buildings*, vol iii (1936)

11 15 Car.II., c.1 (1663)

12 6 Ann., c.4, Fornhill to Stony Stratford; 6 Ann., c.77, Old Stratford to Dunchurch (1706-7)

13 See the Gazetteer for references to all Leicestershire and Rutland Acts

14 Daniel Defoe, *A Tour through England and Wales*, (Everyman Edition, 1928) p.117

15 Ibid, vol ii p 118

16 Ibid, vol ii p 128

17 Gazetteer No.3

18 William Marshall, *Rural Economy of the Midland Counties* (1796), vol i p 49

19 Gazetteer No 17

20 Op cit, vol i p 35

21 John Monk, *General View of the Agriculture of the County of Leicester* (1794) pp 53-4

22 Gazetteer No 1. For a note on the Chain Bridge, see E Jervoise, *The Ancient Bridges of Mid and Eastern England* (1932) p.61

23 Gazetteer No.2

24 Gazetteer No.4

25 Gazetteer No.4

26 Gazetteer No.5

27 Percy Russell, *A Leicestershire Road* (1934)

28 Statutorily deposited under 3 Geo.IV, c.126 (1822)

29 1 Geo.IV, c.95 (1820)

30 13 Geo.I, c.12 (1726-7)

31 Gazetteer No.4 and Map 2

32 Gazetteer No.12 and Map 3

33 Gazetteer No.11

34 Gazetteer No. 8

35 Gazetteer No. 9

36 Gazetteer No.12

37 Gazetteer No.14

38 Gazetteer No.15

39 Gazetteer No. 28

40 Gazetteer No. 30

41 See Arthur Cossons, *The Turnpike Roads of Nottinghamshire* (1934) [republished by Nottinghamshire County Council, 1994]

42 Daniel Defoe, op cit,II, p119 et seq

43 Samuel Smiles, *Lives of the Engineers* (1861)

44 55 Geo.III., c.152 (1815)

45 Commenced 1818, opened 1826

46 J.L.McAdam, *Remarks on the Present System of Roadmaking*, 7th edition (1823), p.111

47 Sir Henry Parnell, *A Treatise on Roads* (1833), p.74

48 See Roy Devereux, *John Loudon McAdam* (1936), for details of the family

49 7 Geo.IV, c.cxlii (1826)

50 Paterson's *Roads*, 15th edition (1811)

51 Charles Knight, *British Almanac* (1836)

52 Ibid (1837) (See figure 24 on page 38)

53 Ibid (1838)

54 Opened 1837 under the Act 3-4 Wm.IV, c.xxxiv (1832-4)

55 Opened 1830 under the Act 7 Geo.IV, c.xlix (1826)

56 Opened 1832 under the Act 11 Geo.IV and 1 Wm IV, c.lviii (1830-1)

57 For example, the Ashby to Ticknall line, with branches, serving the lime works on the Derbyshire border, and the Duke of Rutland's private line connecting Belvoir Castle with the Grantham Canal near Muston. There had also been a line joining the ill-starred Charnwood Forest Canal at Nanpantan to Loughborough

58 Under the Act 6-7 Wm.IV, c.lxxviii

59 Ordinance of 31 Mar 1654 with amendment of 2 Sep 1654

60 14 Car.II, c.6 (1662)

61 22 Car.II, c.12 (1670)

62 7-8 Wm.III, c.29 (1695-6)

63 6 Ann., c.56 (c.29 in Ruffhead's edition)

64 5 Geo.I, c.12 (1719)

65 14 Geo.II, c.42 (1741)

66 21 Geo.II, c.28 (1748)

67 24 Geo.II, c.43 (1751)

68 26 Geo.II, c.30 (1753)

69 28 Geo.II, c.17 (1755)

70 5 Geo.III, c.38 (1765)

71 14 Geo.III, c.82 (1774) This was a 5 years' extension of a year's exemption given by 13 Geo.III, c.84

72 Sharp's 'Rolling Waggon' for eight horses and 'rolling Carts' for two or four oxen were advertised, with illustrations, in 1773

73 The seventeenth century had an omnibus word 'horsebeast', that covered 'mare', 'gelding', etc.

74 See feature box on p.19

75 For example, J. Bateman, *The General Turnpike Roads Acts*, various editions

76 See feature box on p.24

77 In this it differed from the usual toll bridge which was erected and owned by a company of proprietors. See feature box on pp26-27

78 5-6 Wm.IV, c.50

79 1-2 Wm.IV, c.6 With the exception of 1832 and 1833, there was an act in this series every year to 1884-5 (48-9 Vic., c.37)

80 Samuel Bagshaw, *History, Gazetteer and Directory of Derbyshire* (1846)

81 By 14-15 Vic.,c.38 Annual Acts down to 1872 (35-6 Vic., c.72), except in 1868-9 and 1871

82 The statistics for 1834 and 1839 are from Charles Knight, *British Almanac* (1842) and those for 1837 and 1849 from the 1853 edition of the same work

83 The measurements used for the graph in figure 12 were worked out on modern maps. Discrepancies between them and the figures given here may be due to differences in the allotting of shares of border roads, to the difficulty of judging for what distance the routes from Leicester were administered by the street commissioners, and some roads not officially disturnpiked may have been treated as lapsed.

84 The 'A road' numbers used are those shown in The Automobile Association, *The Illustrated Road Book of England & Wales*. (2nd post-war edition, 1958)

Index